ON MY WAY

On My Way

The View from the Ninth Decade

Daniel Hertzler

Foreword by
David B. Miller

DreamSeeker Books
TELFORD, PENNSYLVANIA

an imprint of
Cascadia Publishing House

Cascadia Publishing House orders, information, reprint permissions:
contact@CascadiaPublishingHouse.com
1-215-723-9125
126 Klingerman Road, Telford PA 18969
www.CascadiaPublishingHouse.com

On My Way
Copyright © 2013 by Cascadia Publishing House LLC
Telford, PA 18969
All rights reserved
DreamSeeker Books is an imprint of Cascadia Publishing House LLC
Library of Congress Catalog Number: 2013008417
ISBN 13: 978-1-931038-96-6; **ISBN 10:** 1-931038-96-1
Book design by Cascadia Publishing House
Cover design by Dawn Ranck

The paper used in this publication is recycled and meets the
minimum requirements of American National Standard for Information Sciences—
Permanence of Paper for Printed Library Materials, ANSI Z39.48-1984.1984

Library of Congress Cataloguing-in-Publication Data
Hertzler, Daniel.
 On my way : the view from the ninth decade / Daniel Hertzler.
  pages cm
 Includes bibliographical references.
 Summary: "This book is one part theological reflection, one part memoir, one part critique of American transportation plus various other observations on this and that" "[summary]"--Provided by publisher.
 ISBN 978-1-931038-96-6 (pbk. : alk. paper) -- ISBN 1-931038-96-1 (pbk. : alk. paper)
 1. Hertzler, Daniel. 2. Editors--United States--Biography. 3. Mennonites--United States--Biography. I. Title.
 BX8143.H47A3 2013
 289.7092--dc23
 [B]
                                        2013008417

20 19 18 17 16 15 14 13   10 9 8 7 6 5 4 3 2 1

To Mary,
who read and approved while it was being written

Contents

Foreword by David B. Miller 9
Author's preface 11

1 Still writing checks • 15
2 In the beginning, God • 22
3 Jesus Christ as Lord • 30
4 On a committee • 37
5 I married a preacher's daughter • 43
6 A house by the side of a country road • 55
7 Gardening 101 • 61
8 A beekeeper must pay attention • 69
9 Transportation follies • 75
10 As I was saying • 83
11 And so on... • 90

Appendixes
    A. Our family 94
    B. Incomplete list of Mary's flowers 95
    C. Vehicles we have owned 97
Notes 99
The Author 102

Foreword

I don't recall the first time that I met Dan Hertzler. I do know that well before our first face to face introduction, I had come to know him through his weekly editorials in the *Gospel Herald*, at that time the news and features magazine of the Mennonite Church. For this newcomer among Mennonites, Dan's columns became a short course on how this community of faith engaged in a living conversation between the meaning of its confession and the living of life in this world. Dan's columns, whether musing on decisions facing the church or current global events, persistently, patiently, and humbly probed the question of how we follow Christ in this time and place.

Coming from a triumphal version of mainline Christianity that had not yet recognized the impending demise of Christendom, I found the character of Dan's writing both striking and instructive. His words were typically understated, made colorful by a wry sense of humor, and used to tell truthful, modest—rather than inflated, heroic—stories about ourselves. In a culture where Christian faith is often turned into a commodity and marketing strategy, Dan taught me to value the community of faith that is—to remain restless for greater faithfulness but never to disdain the fallible nor to make too great a claim for our achievement. Long before Brian McLaren wrote his book, Dan demonstrated the nature of a "generous orthodoxy." Inherent in his writing was (and is) a leaning toward trust in God rather than certitude.

Now, in a second memoir focused primarily on life beyond his professional work, Dan uses words with that same character.

Each chapter traces an element of life over time—be it reading the Bible, building a home, keeping bees or a garden. In Garrison Keillor-esque fashion, Dan introduces a theme then invites us on narrative walk and brings each stroll through time and experience back home to lessons learned and hope that endures.

Deeply embedded in this memoir is the story of life with his soul mate, Mary. From naive meeting—"a girl in the college library caught my attention. How does it happen? It is a mystery, but there she was in the library"—then follows the story of a journey together, a lesson in fidelity and uncommon love in the commonplace. Like the shared task of gardening the story is patient, persistent, fruitful.

There is joy, deep prizing of his Mary, and yes, sorrow. For this is truth-telling. Dan does not sensationalize trauma but poignantly gives us a glimpse of the sadness late in life's journey, the onset of dementia for Mary. "The house is empty without her despite its being filled with her artwork and handiwork." Yet goodness remains, a sixtieth anniversary celebrated in the face of decline—gathering families, photos, memories—summed up with the simple doxology, "A good time was had by all."

Years after Dan and I first met in person, along with longtime friend, Carl Keener, we went to hear the French philosopher Jacques Derrida speak on the Penn State campus. After enduring a three-hour lecture that deconstructed the history of Western civilization and knowing, Dan, with what I had come to prize as a slightly sardonic grin, summed up the evening: "Well I guess words can't mean anything anymore."

Gratefully, Dan did not give up on words! He has written here story and testimony—not as one seeking to make a great universal claim but rather writing as a witness (which even Derrida would appreciate) to faithfulness, foibles, fidelity, and love. Dan has once again offered us words that are modest, truthful, engaging, and wise.

—*David B. Miller, Elkhart, Indiana, is Associate Professor of Missional Leadership Development, Anabaptist Mennonite Biblical Seminary*

Author's preface

Why write a memoir? Especially, why write a second memoir? My earlier one, *A Little Left of Center*, was published in 2000. It highlighted my family background and my professional life. What more can be said? Quite a bit if I would find the energy to pull it together.

On occasion when I meet old friends, they ask what I am "doing." Others are more specific: "What are you writing?" Well of course, as editor of *Gospel Herald* from 1973 to 1990, I used to write nearly every week. Perhaps this memoir is to demonstrate that I can still write.

I hope the following variations on a theme will provide a unified message. We composers of memoirs write partly to justify ourselves. This volume might be characterized as a confession: a confession of faith; a confession of accomplishments; and especially in the chapters on housing and transportation, a confession of involvement with some systems that probably do not have long-term durability. They are based on environmental exploitation that is not sustainable.

I acknowledge that I have been a part of this losing battle over the natural resources. I hope that solutions will be found to the environmental dilemmas and that human life on this planet may continue, but the signals are not all hopeful. Some who would be in a position to do something about the problem resist the evidence, and others are distracted by what seem to them to be more pressing problems.

In the meantime people of faith are invited to present the good news and to accompany this with responsible efforts to protect the environment. I hope they will respond to these opportunities.

—*Daniel Hertzler*
  Scottdale, Pennsylvania

On My Way

Chapter 1

Still writing checks

In 1997 I wrote an article for the *Gospel Herald* titled "When our earthly accounts are closed." I suggested that "life is like a checking account with a limited balance. Year by year we draw on that balance, and eventually nothing remains. The system goes bankrupt." But I added that "people of faith assume that when the earthly account is closed for lack of funds, another will open with full support."[1]

As I write this 15 years later, I am reminded that the check-writing analogy has become dated. Not all of our payments are made by check. But the funds are still taken from an account, so part of the analogy remains.

I seem to remember that when I was about 40, a physician took my blood pressure and predicted I would live to be a hundred. He was a specialist to whom I had taken one of our sons because of an ear problem. I have no documentation of this event but have it stored for whatever perspective it can provide.

I do find that I am in reasonable health—not perfect health, but reasonable. My arms and my legs still work fairly well. A friend whose husband recently died from a disabling illness once remarked that my good health is a "gift," and indeed it is. My mother, Susan Shenk, died of pneumonia at 37; and my father, Melvin Hertzler, died of cancer at 70.

Yet there have been persons in my family who have lived long. My father's younger brother, Milford, lived into his 90s, and Aunt Ida Powell was 104. Indeed, without benefit of modern medicine, our patriarch Jacob Hertzler lived to be 83 in the eighteenth century.

What is the point of a long life? Is one considered a success by simply breathing? What sort of "checks" am I still writing? Once in a while someone stands up, declaims on the issue of "being" versus "doing," and suggests that being is more important than doing. I have never found a way to sort out this proposed contrast. It may be because throughout my life there has been an emphasis on doing.

Beginning at about the age of six, when I was expected to carry wood for the kitchen range, there have been things to do. The tasks were perceived as important, if not by others, then I myself assumed their importance. If I can do the job, why not?

I have been formally retired for more than two decades and thus have some opportunity to choose what I do. Some things must be done for the maintenance of life. Others are optional. When I used to be asked what I am "doing," I would begin, "I walk the dog," but then the dog died.

One of my current mainstays is my work as instructor for the second unit in the five-unit Pastoral Studies Distance Education correspondence course, a college-level training program for students who are not able to attend a residential seminary. This unit is on "The Biblical Story."

Recently I faced this question again and replied, "I'm writing another memoir," which seemed satisfactory. When I reflect on the eight decades of my life (plus some years), I ask myself, "What events are worth describing?" As mentioned in the preface, I have already written *A Little Left of Center*,[2] which highlights my family background and professional life. But there has been more to my life than my profession even though it sometimes seemed all-encompassing. In this memoir I will seek to avoid repeating myself.

I realize that I have lived through the last three-quarters of the twentieth century, described by Isaiah Berlin (1909-97) as the "most terrible century in Western history."[3] In what ways did I experience and/or respond to these momentous events?

No doubt Berlin had in mind the two world wars, the Great Depression, and also the Holocaust. My approach throughout my life has been to seek to cope with whatever comes my way and, it would seem, to stay out of trouble. If I need any justification for this approach, perhaps it can be found in what John Howard Yoder writes in one of his essays: "Who is in high office or what laws are written," he declares, are less important "than the cumulation of an infinity of tiny deeds: mothers who feed their children, children who learn their lessons, craftsmen who finish a job, doctors who get the dosage right, drivers who stay on the road, policemen who hold their fire."[4]

Yoder was arguably the most important Mennonite theologian of my generation, but he operated in a tradition that for more than four centuries has had an uneasy relationship with governments. As I was growing up, we spoke of "nonconformity to the world" on the basis of Romans 12:2. People in our tradition have been taking a stand or moving away to be able to practice our convictions. The issues have been particularly focused in times of war. My own destiny has been affected by both World Wars I and II even though I did not directly participate in either one.

Without the U.S. involvement in World War I, my father might well have been a teacher instead of a farmer. After one year in college, he went back to the farm to avoid the military draft. If he had been a teacher, it would no doubt have changed my experience in World War II. As it turned out, I was deferred from the draft to help my father on the farm instead of going into Civilian Public Service, which I would have found more interesting. The Smoke Jumpers, for example, would have been much more exciting than milking cows and forking manure.

I have memories of the Great Depression—not comprehensive memories, but a few anecdotes. The year 1931, I think it was, my father described as "the year of the drought." As a result, he and my uncle Milford, who operated the farm owned by their mother, needed to buy extra feed for the cattle. Then came deflation, and as Dad reported, they had to pay for it with deflated dollars. But the Elverson (Pa.) National Bank did not fail, and life went on. Food was plentiful, with quite a bit produced right on the farm. I also remember that we could buy unwrapped bread delivered to the farm for five cents a loaf.

My father did not receive a newspaper, so our knowledge of world events was limited. I recall, however, that I found an Alf Landon campaign button on the road in 1936, when he was the Republican candidate for president. The button had a cloth sunflower backing since he was from Kansas. Landon was soundly defeated by F. D. Roosevelt although Roosevelt was not popular with farmers. Our neighbor, Reg Smith, passed on a joke about Roosevelt. He was likened to Christopher Columbus: "When he started out, he didn't know where he was going. When he got there, he didn't know where he was. And he traveled on borrowed money." For myself, I remember that Roosevelt advocated for Social Security, and numbers of us today depend on it.

I learned about Pearl Harbor on Sunday evening at church (December 7, 1941). That attack was followed by Roosevelt's "Day of Infamy" speech and a declaration of war. The war was to overshadow my life for the next four years. World War II has been characterized by some as the "Good War." From the perspective of the Mennonite church, there is no such thing. Numbers of veterans would hold the same opinion. Farley Mowat, a Canadian, published *And No Birds Sang* in 1979, thirty-five years after his experience in the Italian campaign. In "An Anti-Epilogue" he says, "I wrote this book in the absolute conviction that there never has been, nor ever can be, a 'good' or worthwhile war."[5]

As a church we already knew this, and when the United States began to draft soldiers even before Pearl Harbor, Mennonite church leaders negotiated an alternative. So when I became eighteen in 1943, I registered as a conscientious objector, with support from my father and help from our minister, Christian J. Kurtz.

About the same time, Guy F. Hershberger published *War, Peace, and Nonresistance* (1944), which spelled out a theological and sociological position against war. I read his book and found it important, but since I was deferred to work on the farm, the issue did not come into focus.

When Harry Truman brought back the military draft in the late 1940s, I was majoring in Bible at Eastern Mennonite College, and so I could be deferred as a theological student. In 1960 I was ordained to the ministry in the same year our fourth son was born. After this I was able to reduce taxes by counting some income as a ministerial housing allowance, which was thus not taxed.

I use the long form in reporting our income and deduct housing expenses. Since then my wife, Mary, and I have paid little if any federal income tax, much of which goes for military expenditures. I know this has no effect on the ability of the United States to engage in war, but I take satisfaction from being able to direct some of the savings into contributions to the church.

I find it remarkable that national leaders are so successful in arousing public opinion in support of war and rallying the most virile young men to go out and kill or be killed. In "The Birth of War," R. Brian Ferguson reviews archaeological records and concludes that "warfare is largely a development of the past 10,000 years." He finds "a certain ironic logic, given recent events, that the regular practice of warfare that has continued without interruption down to the present began about 10,000 years ago in what is now Northern Iraq." He concludes that "leaders often favor war because war favors leaders."[6]

Chris Hedges poses the question from the soldier's point of view. In *War Is a Force That Gives Us Meaning*, he proposes: "Even with its destruction and carnage, it can give us what we long for in life. It can give us purpose, meaning, a reason for living. . . . It gives us resolve, a cause. It allows us to be noble."[7] This may help to explain the sentiment in the barbershop where I sat during the buildup to the Iraq War (2003-11). The opinion appeared to be about twenty to one in favor of the war. I kept my mouth shut.

In writing I became a little bolder. When *Newsweek* published an article seeming to imply that Europeans were against war in Iraq because they were essentially non-Christian and Americans supported it as Christians, I sent a brief note: "Not all American Christians are fundamentalists who applaud Bush's religious clichés. Some of us are against war because we are Christians."[8]

The 2009 inauguration of Barack Obama as forty-fourth president of the United States caused me some mixed feelings. On the one hand, it was a great relief to see George W. Bush retired. I never had any faith in him although it has been reported that toward the end of his presidency, he made some political moves that were more astute than his earlier blustering rhetoric. I found it encouraging that a majority of voters elected a man who campaigned for change and immediately began to undo some of the antisocial and anti-environmental policies of the Bush administration.

On the other hand, I recognize that Obama represents what Walter Wink describes as *The Powers That Be* (1998) in his book by that name. Regardless of his good intentions, Obama aspired to the office of Commander in Chief and inherited the task of prosecuting two wars left over from the previous administration. He is a member of the United Church of Christ (UCC). One branch of this tradition goes back to the Puritans, who are shown in history books as carrying their guns on the way to church. They did not seem to differentiate between the church and society. In *A People's History of the United States*, Howard Zinn tells of how the Massachusetts Bay Colony hanged Mary Dyer "along with two other Quakers, for 'rebellion, sedition, and presumptuous obtruding themselves.'"[9]

The UCC today is much more astute than this and has theologians such as Walter Brueggemann, who are able to clarify the issues sharply. But the general Christian consensus in this country has been to support a war if the president wants it. This cannot be what Jesus and the early church had in mind. We have not done well in promoting an alternative to this.

The Christian church is an international body, and it could have a major influence if it would exercise its option. As John Stoner once put it, "Let the Christians of the world agree that they will not kill one another." But even here there is hesitation. In 1991 the World Council of Churches met in Canberra, Australia, and took an action opposing all war. But they rescinded it before the assembly was over.

Nevertheless, I take courage from the worldwide distribution of Mennonites. We are a very small denomination, with less than two million members, but we are present in eighty countries. In 2000 PBS broadcast a documentary on conscientious objection in World War II, *The Good War and Those Who Refused to Fight It*. Compared to the millions who went to war, conscientious objectors (COs) were a very small group. Yet at the program's end, a CO named William Roberts shared valuable insight:

> Was our protest and our witness of any benefit to society? Perhaps the answer lies in the findings of the new science of chaos and complexity which has discovered that something as apparently insignificant as the fluttering of a butterfly's wings can trigger a cascade of events that, in due time, affects the weather halfway around the globe. We flapped our butterfly wings in prison. Who can know their effect in our interconnected world?[10]

When one sets out to write a memoir, there is some freedom in deciding what to include. As I have already demonstrated, not all of what I write will be documented. What follows will be in some parts a confession of faith, in other places it will be reporting, and sometimes it will be observations and opinions. Here are things I have seen and heard. Here is what makes sense to me, in some cases what I may hope for but have not been able to realize. And I am still writing checks.

Chapter 2

In the beginning, God

I learned to believe in God from the family and church community in eastern Pennsylvania where I grew up. Piety was important to us, and our piety was based on the Bible.

The Bible we used was the King James. However, Bishop John S. Mast could also read from the German Bible, which included the Apocrypha. This is a series of Jewish writings eventually rejected by Jewish rabbis and Protestants, so they do not appear in most current copies of the King James Version.

Once I heard Bishop Mast comment that the Apocrypha was not considered "inspired" but was "good reading." It was some years before I took the time to examine the Apocrypha. Some of the material in it is quite fanciful, but I found the story of Susanna and the elders to be good reading. Probably a folktale, but good reading.

I began to read the Bible at the age of eight or ten. Our Sunday school had a Bible reading program, and I entered it. The knowledge gained from this and various other experiences with the Bible has served me well. If I have in mind a phrase from the King James Version anywhere in the Bible, I can find it with the help of *Strong's Concordance*.

This version remains in the back of my mind, but I seldom read it today. Two issues call for newer versions: developments of the English language and scholarly efforts to find the most authentic manuscripts of the original texts. The New Revised Standard Version is the Bible I generally carry.

The Bible is a wide-ranging collection of literary productions written over a period of about a thousand years and collected by people who took the writings seriously enough to save them. The question of what sort of literature it is and how to interpret it provides occasion for ongoing debate.

The Bible begins with what appears to be a poetic reflection or perhaps a liturgy for use in a worship service. Modernity sought to turn this into a historical account. Famous among those who helped to distort the interpretation was Archbishop James Ussher (1581-1656), whose *Annals of the World* dated creation at 4004 BC.[11]

No doubt many continue to believe this fiction, perhaps partly because it was carried in notes added to Bibles. My own perspective on this has been modified by comments here and there from persons who seem to know what they are talking about. In 1957 the biblical archaeologist W. F. Albright was a visiting professor at Pittsburgh Theological Seminary and gave a series of public lectures.

Two of his ideas have stayed in my mind. One is that in Genesis 1 is "a truer truth than a literal truth." I find this an interesting observation. A second remark of his was that Noah's flood may have been caused by melting ice after the Ice Age, which raised the sea level several hundred feet. Several recent books by scientists have supported this view. Ian Wilson reports that there are flood stories throughout the world.

More specifically, a Babylonian flood tale has been found that closely resembles the story of Noah. After reviewing the work of scientists who have studied the evidence, Wilson concludes, "Thanks to the science of radio-carbon dating, the time at which this Flood event occurred can now be calculated with very reasonable precision as c. 5600 B.C., that is, during the Late Stone Age."[12]

This does not mean that we need to invoke scientific criteria every time we interpret the biblical text. But we do well to recognize that the biblical authors wrote for their own times, and the compilers did the same. We may profit from their perspective in their own contexts as we seek to address our own setting.

Also, we can find a kind of primitive science in Genesis 1. The writer perceives that God created a "firmament," or "dome," to separate the upper waters from the lower waters. We know that the sky is not a dome. But if we have ever lain on our backs on a clear summer day and looked at the sky, it looks like a dome. The writer of Genesis 1 was an observer.

The writer was also a theologian. We notice in the account that light is created on the first day, but the sun and the moon not until the fourth day, and that their purpose is particularly to "be for seasons and for days and years."[13] So these lights are simply functional—nothing more. It is my understanding that numbers of people in those days worshipped the sun and the moon. The Hebrew theologian would have none of this. As Albright puts it, there is "a truer truth than literal truth."

I once read a humorous article in *His* magazine written as if a letter from a book editor to the author of the Bible and explaining why they could not publish it: too much sex and violence. This memory comes to me sometimes when our Sunday school gives Bibles to fourth graders with the hope that they will read them. But what about one arcane law after another in Leviticus?

When they get through these, what will they do with the violence in Judges? Especially in chapter 19, about the man whose "concubine" had been abused to death; he cut her body into twelve pieces "and sent her throughout all the territory of Israel."[14]

This gruesome line seems not to have impressed me as a young reader. It has been only as an adult that the unsavory aspects of the biblical story have concerned me. Yet I perceive that this is our story, and we need to accept it. The effort to discard the Old Testament was defeated long ago.

As described by John W. Miller in *How the Bible Came to Be*, during the second century a church leader named Marcion tried to get rid of the Hebrew Bible because he held that the God of Israel and the God of Jesus were not the same God. His thesis was rejected and, as Miller reports,

"Israel's Scriptures, likewise revered and preserved on scrolls (but in Greek translation), were transcribed onto the pages of a codex (book), to which were added (in the same codex) certain Christian apostolic writings (also in Greek), thus creating what amounted to a new artifact: an extremely large, single-volume canon-codex made up of translated Jewish Scriptures with apostolic Christian writings added."[15]

This is essentially the Bible we Christians have today.

How to deal with such a wide-ranging and diverse set of literary productions has been a challenge for the church ever since. On the one hand, many statements in the Bible leap out at us and call for attention: "Go to the ant, thou sluggard; consider her ways and be wise."[16] The point seems to be obvious. On the other hand, quotations such as the one above from Judges do not help us unless interpreted in context.

Some interpretations of the Bible are too crass, some are sentimental, and some lessons from the Bible are ignored because readers do not take time to consider them. In his book *Unleashing the Scripture*, Stanley Hauerwas holds that "literalist-fundamentalism and the critical approaches to the Bible are but two sides of the same coin, insofar as each assumes that the texts should be accessible to anyone without the necessary mediation by the church."[17]

Hauerwas is adept at challenging widely accepted assumptions. The subtitle of his book is *Freeing the Bible from Captivity in America*. The quote and the subtitle indicate his concern, and my own experience tends to support it. I remember that the one-room school I attended had images of Washington and Lincoln covering the front of the room above the blackboards.

Our day began with a reading of ten verses of Scripture by the teacher, recital of the Lord's Prayer in the Anglican version, salute to the American flag, and singing one verse of the song "America." This sanctified patriotism tended not to impress me because my family and church community had a perspective that differed from it.

As I have reported above, my view of the Bible and its interpretation has been modified since then, but I perceive that the tradition as I have come to understand it is based on a foundation laid down in an Amish Mennonite community in eastern Pennsylvania.

I do have one odd memory of an interpretation of Scripture that was off the mark. In those days it was a practice to hold a public meeting on Sunday evening during which laypersons of the congregation were invited to help interpret Scripture and suggest the implications.

On one occasion John J. Stoltzfus was assigned a topic including Romans 12:11a, which in the King James Version reads, "Not slothful in business." He concluded that Paul was encouraging vigor in business practice. John did not recognize that language changes and that a current reading would be more like the NRSV, a more general encouragement, "Do not lag in zeal." That leads the rest of the verse into "Be ardent in spirit, serve the Lord."[18]

I cannot say that his reading a pro-business interpretation out of the Bible was really harmful to us. The speaker was a farmer and not in the position to do widespread harm based on a misinterpretation of the text. But it is a reminder that interpretation of Scripture is a delicate exercise, as highlighted by *The Art of Reading Scripture*, edited by Ellen F. Davis and Richard B. Hays.

This book is the result of a four-year "conversation" among biblical scholars. The introduction reports that "in the course of our consultation, the conviction grew among us that reading Scripture is an art—a creative discipline that requires engagement and imagination, in contrast to the Enlightenment's ideal of a detached objectivity."

Among the important observations in the book is one by Ellen F. Davis:

> The most difficult aspect of the Bible's literary complexity is its use of symbols. The Bible speaks often in symbolic, or imaginative, language for the simple reason that

the realities of which it speaks exceed the capacity of ordinary "commonsense" discourse.[19]

Although the pro-business interpretation of Romans 12:11a by John J. Stoltzfus probably did no great harm, some distorted interpretations of Scripture have done harm by promoting a mind-set alien to the message of Scripture and sometimes even by adding that perspective to the printed Bible. One of the most notorious is the dispensational theory of an Englishman, John Nelson Darby. His interpretation was popularized by the American C. I. Scofield and inserted into the *Scofield Reference Bible* (1909, rev. 1917), still available in bookstores today.

This dispensational theory is evidently the source of the theology for the Left Behind series of adventure novels published by Tyndale Press. These novels interpret literally just about every violent image in the book of Revelation. The authors' failure to comprehend the symbolism in Revelation has provided a distorted interpretation, which serves to reinforce the violence among many American Christians who are not prepared to endorse the position of Jesus, who said, "Love your enemies."[20]

For myself, the rule of thumb in biblical interpretation is the inductive method. It asks three questions: (1) What does the text say? (2) What did it mean in its own time? (3) What is its significance today? This is no foolproof method, but it seeks to take the text seriously and opens the way for *The Second Naiveté*, as described by Mark I. Wallace in his book by that title.

Wallace proposes that

> a hermeneutic of the second naiveté will focus on the give-and-take between text and audience; it will maintain that Scripture is more like a lively and open-ended game between its world and the world of the reader than it is a closed book whose meaning is exhausted by the standard theological Lexicon.[21]

I find Wallace comforting and hope that I may be standing with him.

If I am ever challenged in this position regarding the Bible, I would have one more comment. This perspective is developed by Nancey Murphy in *Anglo-American Postmodernity*. Murphy reports that after Descartes the prevailing philosophy became "foundationalism," which held that any position one takes must be built on a solid foundation section by section up to the present.

But, as Murphy reports, this has not been found logically possible. We cannot start at the bottom because we all begin with our own assumptions. One would think that it should not have taken several hundred years to recognize this inadequacy, but so it goes.

Murphy observes that philosophers today tend to favor "holism," recognizing "a complex mutual conditioning between parts and whole. It recognizes different levels of complexity and recognizes as well that no one level can be thoroughly understood in isolation from its neighbors."[22] So we all operate from within our own tradition. My tradition assumes that God was in the beginning, is now, and ever shall be. Within that tradition we test the reality we experience and seek to devise appropriate responses.

The Bible begins with a garden and ends with a city. Some of us as gardeners can identify with the garden. When we are feeling honest, we can even perceive the dilemma of the hapless couple who aimed to be sophisticated but ended by losing it all.

The city is another matter. It is like one we have never seen, and there seems to be a tendency to push it ahead and up into the sky. I find it remarkable that in the popular culture people who have died are perceived to have gone up and are looking down. But in Revelation 21 the holy city keeps "coming down."

John in his vision is evidently seeing the church as the city of God, with its doors open to invite everyone in. This is a remarkable vision, perhaps too comprehensive a vision for us.

Rather than accept it as our own, it seems easier to kick it into the future or turn it into some literalistic distortion.

If John the Revelator is too much for us, there is the philosopher-theologian who wrote the letter of 1 John and observes that "no one has ever seen God." But then he asserts that "if we love one another, God lives in us, and his love is perfected in us." He adds that "God abides in those who confess that Jesus is the Son of God, and they abide in God." Also, "God is love, and those who abide in love abide in God, and God abides in them."[23]

At first glance maybe this does not seem as impressive as foundationalism once seemed, but it offers a place to stand from which to view the passing scene and, as John insists, to practice our faith in God.

Chapter 3

Jesus Christ as Lord

In 1962 Karl Barth visited America to lecture at Princeton Theological Seminary and the University of Chicago. On that trip he was asked for a summary of his theology and replied:

> Jesus loves me, this I know,
> > For the Bible tells me so.

This is a remarkable summary by a famous theological wordsmith (1886-1968). Theologians are given to multiplying words, so asking them to simplify is fair. On the other hand, simplifying runs the risk of distortion.

The ditty is all right for children in light of Mark 10:14, where Jesus is quoted as saying, "Let the children come to me; do not stop them." But for adults this is only half a gospel. The accounts of Jesus' interaction with adults indicate that he expected something from them.

What we know and believe about Jesus has been culturally transmitted to us. There is no way to completely bypass two thousand years of tradition in our effort to understand what it means to follow Jesus. Yet we are called upon to reject obvious distortions. James William McClendon Jr. wrote of the context in which Clarence Jordan developed Koinonia Farm, an interracial community:

> Jordan lived in a region where Jesus was a mantric charm, where "the blood" was proclaimed by radio evangelists and crossroad preachers as patent medicine effective without cost or obligation to the taker—and yet

where militarism, materialism, and racism continued to grind Black faces and White ones into the Southern dust.[24]

McClendon himself grew up in a similar culture and had a second conversion through reading John Howard Yoder's *The Politics of Jesus*. He declared:

> That book changed my life. . . . Night and day I read through the *Politics*, and by the time I had finished, I had undergone a second conversion, not as at my baptism merely to follow Jesus, but now to follow Jesus this way—Jesus interpreted by Yoder's scornful passion to overcome standard-account thinking.[25]

The point Yoder made, as I understand it, is that Jesus' example and teaching are relevant for us today. This is no new idea for Mennonites. Yoder just put it into theological terms. As we may have noticed, the so-called Apostles' Creed fails to mention the life and teaching of Jesus. It goes directly from "born of the Virgin Mary" to "suffered under Pontius Pilate." Although this is number 712 in *Hymnal: A Worship Book* (1992), I seldom hear it used in a Mennonite worship service.

Instead, we seek to cherish the Sermon on the Mount, a summary of Jesus' teaching appearing in Matthew 5 to 7. The late Bishop John E. Lapp from Franconia Mennonite Conference once observed that this sermon had been used as instructional material when his wife was prepared for baptism. It must have been effective, he said, because "she is a better Christian than I am."

For myself, to have Jesus as example and teacher is a challenge. Where Jesus was reportedly confrontational, I am retiring. From the Gospels we learn that he was crucified because he threatened the powers. I generally try to keep out of trouble.

Some years ago I memorized the first chapter of the Gospel of Mark. It starts out, "The beginning of the good news of Jesus Christ, the Son of God." Each noun in this sentence is loaded with meaning. A little further, in verses 14 and 15, Mark reports that Jesus came to Galilee and asserted, "The time is fulfilled, and the kingdom of God has come near; repent, and believe in the good news."

What was Jesus calling for? Yoder observes:

> It hardly needs to be argued that "kingdom" is a political term; the common Bible reader is less aware that "gospel" as well means not just any old welcome report, but the kind of publicly important proclamation that is worth sending with a runner and holding a celebration for when it is received.[26]

As the Gospels all show, Jesus did not intend to carry out his mission alone: he enlisted a dozen apostles. What he and they were seeking to do so rattled the establishment that they could do nothing less than have Jesus put away. His efforts were cut off by his death as a common criminal. Yet each of the four Gospels affirms that he was raised again, and the book of Acts describes the ongoing efforts of the early followers.

Nevertheless Jesus' untimely death was a problem that the early Christians had to deal with. Before the Gospels were available, the apostle Paul wrestled with the issue in writing to the Corinthians. "Christ crucified," he writes, is "a stumbling block to Jews and foolishness to Gentiles."

Jews expected deeds more than words as a sign that God was on their side. Gentiles wanted a religion that made sense from an intellectual standpoint. "But," Paul insists, "to those who are the called, both Jews and Greeks, Christ the power of God and the wisdom of God."[27]

Debate over the meaning of Jesus' death continues until this day. Paul discusses this also in Romans 5:8: "God proves his love for us in that while we still were sinners Christ died for us." In some respects Paul has become more influential than the writers of the Gospels in the interpretation of Jesus' death. And many have gone beyond Paul.

The conventional view of Jesus' "atonement" seems to be that someone needed to die for our sins. Jesus died, and this opened a way for us to be delivered. This view is described by Joel B. Green and Mark D. Baker as the "penal substitutionary" theory of the atonement. Green and Baker observe that this theory fits the mind-set of Americans because of its emphasis on "guilt and innocence on the one hand, and toward autobiography on the other."[28]

It appears that some among us can think of no other view of the atonement than this one. Yet John Driver in his book *Understanding the Atonement for the Mission of the Church* shows that the New Testament uses multiple images in the effort to interpret the meaning of Jesus' death. He says, "The value of any one of these images depends on allowing it to remain in relationship to all the rest."[29]

I am inclined toward the Christus Victor view of the atonement, which holds that by refusing to retaliate, Jesus defeated the powers lined up against him. As described in Colossians 2:15, "He disarmed the rulers and authorities and made a public display of them, triumphing over them in it."

I think the penal substitutionary theory tends to make us observers rather than participants, so that following Jesus is to assent and not much more. Shane Claiborne addressed the 2009 Mennonite Church USA assembly in Columbus, Ohio, and reflected on his experience with revivalism as a young person: "We came 'just as I am' and left 'just as we were.'"

We do better to stay with the biblical story rather than spend time debating elaborate atonement theories. In Mark 8:34 Jesus says, "If any want to become my followers, let them deny themselves and take up their cross and follow me." For us, the cross is a metaphor, but it makes clear that to follow Jesus is serious business and may well invite opposition.

In their commentaries on Mark, Lamar Williamson Jr. and Timothy Geddert both reflect on this verse and its possible meaning in our time. Thus Williamson writes:

> The significance of this text lies in its paradoxes. I learn who I am by discovering who Jesus is. The way to self-fulfillment is the way of self-denial. . . . The call, the

warning, and the challenge are significant because they cut clean across the grain of conventional wisdom, popular piety, and natural inclination.[30]

Similarly Geddert observes:

> Many church traditions seek their primary definition of the Christian life first and foremost in the writings of Paul.... By beginning with the Gospels, we have the advantage of keeping central the underlying basis for all Christian living: commitment to Jesus Christ and obedience to him.[31]

In his *Reply to False Accusations* (1552), Menno Simons writes that true Christians "seek, desire, and know nothing but peace; and are prepared to forsake country, goods, life, and all for the sake of peace. For they are the kingdom, people, congregation, city, property, and body of peace, as has been heard."[32] Menno himself was an example of one who was prepared to sacrifice on behalf of his calling as a leader among the Anabaptists.

I have lived in a gentler context than he, and my conviction has never been severely tested. Once I did advocate for peace to a roomful of National Rifle Association types, and they were not amused. But generally I have been able to stay in the background.

I tell myself that if worse comes to worst, my intention is to be faithful. If Jesus is to be Lord, we will expect, in Williamson's terms, to reject "conventional wisdom, popular piety, and natural inclination."

Most Christian traditions acknowledge the importance of Jesus' death by their observance of the Lord's Supper, a symbolic mini-meal. This is based on several references in the new Testament, particularly 1 Corinthians 11:26: "As often as you eat this bread and drink the cup, you proclaim the Lord's death until he comes."

In the church community where I grew up, the Supper was observed twice a year and was preceded a week earlier by a congregational meeting. We were expected to scrub our souls and respond to two questions: (1) Are you at peace with God? (2) Are you at peace with your fellow members? No doubt most of the people could respond to these questions readily. For me as an impressionable young member, there was anxiety. I had no enemies as far as I could tell, but as for peace with God, how could I be sure?

The observance of the Supper itself had a distinctive interpretation. All of the women wore black, and the deacon read Isaiah 53 as part of the ritual leading up to the Supper. There was a severity in these practices that I can appreciate as an adult but that as a young person I may have taken too seriously. My experience of the observance of the Supper today is much more informal, perhaps sometimes too informal.

The emphasis on soul-searching was surely based on 1 Corinthians 11:28-29: "Examine yourselves, and only then eat of the bread and drink of the cup. For all who eat and drink without discerning the body, eat and drink judgment on themselves." I think our church leaders had not fully understood the context for these words.

Earlier in the chapter, Paul has complained about the lack of concern for the poor. Richard B. Hays writes that "when Paul speaks of eating the bread and drinking the cup in an unworthy manner (v. 27), he is referring to those who ignore their poorer brothers in the Church."[33]

John Howard Yoder goes further. In chapter 2 of *Body Politics*, he points out that the meaning of the Lord's Supper became distorted by "centuries of ceremonies and arguments about what the ceremonies mean."

Yoder explains that "theologians were concerned in the sixteenth century for detailed theoretical definition of the meaning of certain actions and things called 'Sacraments' with the special set-apart world of the 'religious.'"[34] He reports that in the post-Pentecost church the Lord's Supper was simply a common meal.

So Yoder works out the implications of a common Christian meal: a gathering of a new family based on faith in Jesus.

The meal itself is a worship service, and the implications are to be worked out in all relationships.

In the final section of the chapter, Yoder challenges the so-called "order of creation," according to which "bankers should accumulate money, not share it. . . . Lords should domineer, and soldiers and hangmen should kill, because these are their defined roles in the world."[35] Yoder's answer to this is that the vocation of people with power should be tempered by their calling as Christians.

In the end we are left with the mystery and the paradox of the cross. As Paul has put it to the Corinthians, the cross is "a stumbling block to Jews and foolishness to Gentiles, but to those who are the called, both Jews and Greeks, Christ the power of God and the wisdom of God."[36]

From this some have gone on to construct complicated theories of atonement. I consider it better to go back, as Timothy Geddert urges, to "commitment to Jesus Christ and obedience to him." That is a heavy assignment and worthy of more attention than most of us are prepared to give it.

Chapter 4

On a committee

In spring 2009 Peter J. Dyck (1914-2010) made an odd comment in a Sunday school class. He suggested that the work he and his wife, Elfrieda, had done to direct the migration of some five thousand Mennonite refugees from Europe to Paraguay was not really very much. Someone else had determined that this should be done, and their work was simply to carry out the directive.

Peter was being too modest. As recorded in their book *Up from the Rubble*,[37] Peter and his wife did more than simply carry out orders. But his remark serves as a useful comment on all human efforts. Most of the time most of us do not function alone: whatever we accomplish depends on vision and support from various people.

I have never done anything as dramatic as Peter and Elfrieda. Yet I have been working in the church for some seventy years, beginning as a teenager. I was a paid professional for forty years, as described in my book *A Little Left of Center*,[38] but I also did a lot of voluntary (unpaid) work for the church. Actually, I seldom if ever volunteered for anything. People just asked me to perform tasks that seemed to be important, and I responded to the invitation.

Jo-Ann Brant wrote that she became a Mennonite because the church put her to work. "I walked into the Mennonite church, they put me on a committee, and that was that."[39] For me it was the other way around. I was already part of the church community, and leaders began to give me assignments. My identity has been formed in part by what was expected of me.

My work in the church has generally been in support of a system rather than out in front, pioneering new efforts. But I take comfort from the book of Ephesians: the work of church leaders is "to equip the saints for the work of ministry, for building up the body of Christ."[40] Who is to say how much my volunteer activities contributed to this purpose?

The first assignment I can remember was to serve as Sunday school secretary for the Rock Mennonite Church near Elverson, Pennsylvania. The secretary was expected to order supplies for the Sunday school, and one reason I remember this assignment is that one time I forgot to order the study booklets until it was almost too late. Some of the booklets sent to us were from an imprint edition for a different Mennonite group. The supply of the regular edition had already been exhausted.

This assignment is typical of the sort of work I've generally done for the church: administration and teaching. Most of it was not really exciting, although a few dramatic experiences linger in my mind. In 1952 my wife, Mary, and I moved to Scottdale, Pennsylvania, where I was employed as an assistant editor at Mennonite Publishing House. The local churches were active in teaching, and it was assumed that we as newcomers should be open for assignments.

Alta Mae Erb was in charge of a Wednesday evening educational program, and she saw Mary and me as teachers. Mary was assigned to teach a group of girls, and I had a class of preteen boys. There were no printed curriculum materials. We were expected to provide for these ourselves.

I had spent five years in college, majoring in Bible, but nothing had prepared me for this. Having a roomful of restless, pre-adolescent boys was almost more than I could handle. After one weekly class was over, I would begin to worry about the next. I was too naive and maybe too proud to resign, but it was a great relief when this trial was over.

My adult class version of this experience came twelve or fifteen years later when I was teaching the Men's Bible class at Kingview Mennonite Church. One Harry Rankin was president, secretary, and treasurer of the class and may have thought he should also be the teacher. He followed a regular routine of mild harassment. After I was half or two-thirds through a class, he would say, "Back there you said this. Now you said that. You contradicted yourself." I could never come up with a sharp retort, but none of the other class members seemed interested in the exchange, so it did not really matter.

In the 1960s, Mary and I served as youth sponsors, retiring when our sons who were in the youth group recommended it. On reflection I do not remember that this assignment used my best gifts, but we tried to carry through on what was asked of us.

I think I did better in administrative work involving congregational, district conference, and general church organizations. Sometimes the district and general church activity overlapped with my time as an editor. But Ben Cutrell, general manager of Mennonite Publishing House, supported these assignments because he saw a need for an editor to be involved in other church activities.

A number of terms I served as chair of Kingview Mennonite Church. On the district conference level, I was first drafted as assistant secretary in 1953 to keep the minutes of the annual meeting. As detailed below, I was later to be secretary of the Allegheny Mennonite Mission Board, moderator of the Conference (two stints), and chair of the Leadership Commission. For some twenty-five years I was overseer of one or more Allegheny Conference congregations. The overseer was a liaison between conference and congregations as well as a mentor during periods of pastoral change.

The records of most of these activities are buried in archives. However, some evidence appears in published reports. *Mennonite Yearbook and Directory* shows the following service:
- 1961-66: Secretary, Allegheny Mennonite Mission Board;
- 1967-72: Member, Goshen College Overseers;
- 1973-74: Acting President, Mennonite Board of Education;

- 1981-85: Moderator, Allegheny Mennonite Conference;
- 1988-89: Moderator Elect, Allegheny Mennonite Conference;
- 1989–90: Moderator, Allegheny Mennonite Conference. The *Yearbook* evidently went into an economy mode at this time, did not publish every year, and thus missed recording this term.[41]

For a time I was chair of the Theological and Pastoral Education Council (TPEC) organized by Mennonite Board of Education. Evidence for this is in my file: minutes from what may have been the last meeting of this council, October 29, 2001. Included in the minutes are twelve items, including plans for a next meeting on October 4-5, 2002. I do not believe this meeting was held. The sponsoring agency, Mennonite Board of Education, was replaced by Mennonite Education Agency in the Mennonite reorganization that became Mennonite Church USA (from 2002).

The minutes of the meeting report inside activity and issues that would not make much sense outside the circle of administrators and concerned persons who were present. However, an ongoing legacy of this Council has been Pastoral Studies Distance Education, a five-unit correspondence course on a college level. For more than ten years I have been instructor for this program's second unit, on biblical study. This is not a volunteer assignment: I receive modest compensation for my work as an instructor.

I reported above that the Mennonite Board of Education, which had sponsored TPEC, morphed into the Mennonite Education Agency. Other organizations that I have served have changed or disappeared. The Kingview Mennonite Church, where I volunteered for more than forty years, was merged in 2003 with the Mennonite Church of Scottdale to become the Scottdale Mennonite Church.

The Allegheny Mennonite Conference, which listed 3,752 members when I retired as moderator in 1990, now reports 2,900.[42] Some congregations became concerned over issues that emerged at the time of the formation of Mennonite Church USA and departed for other associations.

Hebrews 13:14 in the King James Version asserts, "Here have we no continuing city, but we seek one to come." In the meantime, life goes on. I cannot say that I'm sorry for supporting these efforts. If they asked me to do something and I could do it, I would give it a try. No one ever dismissed me for incompetence. How could they dismiss a volunteer?

Sometime after I had retired as an editor, I was persuaded to join with Mary as a volunteer at World's Attic in Somerset, Pennsylvania. This thrift (secondhand) store sends its surplus income to support Mennonite Central Committee. We worked there three times a month. I had never thought of myself as a storekeeper, but as a volunteer, why not?

On most days the earnings would defeat a store operated for profit, but with volunteers, the work goes on. We retired from this assignment at the beginning of 2012.

At the 2009 and 2011 assemblies of Mennonite Church USA, Mary and I sat in the visitors' section to observe the delegates at work. We were not out of place. The delegates were less than half the adults who attended the assembly. I had been a congregational delegate to the 2007 assembly, and in my report to my home congregation, I recommended that they send a younger delegate. So they sent a young adult.

We noticed quite a few babies at the assembly, and Mary became concerned, remembering when we (and especially she) wrestled with three boys under three. But I consider the presence of babies at a churchwide meeting a good sign. It shows that young parents are interested in and concerned about our church. We are part of an ongoing tradition.

Nothing we have done was ever enough, but we need not brood over our failures. In *The Rise of Christianity*, Rodney Stark wrote of how the early Christian church prevailed in the Roman Empire. One reason was because Christians preached a God of love. Pagans had no sense that their gods loved them or cared for them.[43]

There are always disruptive forces at work that can bring a church down. But if we can love one another and preach the love of God, we can make a case for the church. Sometime in the 1960s, I think it was, I attended a Christian education seminar in Kentucky. One fellow led a session that caused people to respond with "These are great ideas, but the people back home will not be open to them." The leader reacted vigorously somewhat as follows: "Don't campaign, but be a predictable person."

Is this enough? At some points in the past, radicals have turned things upside down. Should we not try to make a real difference? On reflection, we observe that some of these upsets have been worthwhile, but not all of them. Political irruptions such as the American Revolutionary and Civil Wars have been analyzed by some reflective thinkers as violent solutions to problems that would have been better addressed on a nonviolent basis.

Meanwhile younger persons come into leadership in the church. We see signs of the Spirit at work. Let God be praised.

Chapter 5

I married a preacher's daughter

The mystery of marital bonding is one I will never fully comprehend. Men and women find each other, come together, and may spend more than fifty years as married people. Then again, they may not. How did we stay together?

As much as anything, it was because Mary Yoder and I understood our marriage as permanent. We assumed that marriage is something we undertake as a lifetime commitment. Of course there were supporting factors. Before long our marriage became our security. Also my work and the community where we lived supported it. There was no reason to separate.

The extended buildup to our marriage contributed to the permanence of it. Although I had two sisters, for me girls were a mystery, and I hesitated to get close to one. My perception of our family, at the lower level of the economic community, did not encourage me to "date." I would have hesitated to invite a girl to go to the biweekly Young People's Singing in the farm truck.

My uncle Truman Hertzler wanted to be helpful. "Get yourself an Amish girl," he said. I'm sure he was not thinking of Amish as in Old Order Amish, but of Amish Mennonite such as the Conestoga Amish Mennonite Church near Morgantown, Pennsylvania. I think he did meet Mary before he died. If so, perhaps he could have been reassured to find that she was an Amish Mennonite from northeastern Ohio.

When I went to college at Eastern Mennonite in Harrisonburg, Virginia, there was a whole new context. But I had gone to college to study. One thing at a time. For the first year I made no romantic moves. But by the sophomore year, something told me I should get interested in girls.

A girl in the college library caught my attention. How does it happen? It is a mystery, but there she was in the library. She was Mary Louise Yoder from Mantua, Ohio. Then one evening I found her in the hall and invited her to go with me to the performance of *Messiah* at nearby Bridgewater College.

She agreed, and so we went, riding with Pete Kauffman and his date in his 1938 Chrysler. Three and a half years later we were married. Three and a half years? Why so long? There was a lot to do. For me, to make up my mind. Then to finish school. For Mary, to keep house for her father, Eugene Yoder, after her mother died. And wait for me.

Things began to move after we married—things we could not have anticipated. It is remarkable how naive we were in our mid-twenties. Both of us had gone to college and studied subjects that did not promise professional opportunities. After two years Mary had a junior college Bible certificate, and after five years I had a bachelor of theology degree. I was trained for the ministry, but a professional pastor role was not yet common in my wing of the Mennonite church.

Our lack of occupational urgency may have been related to our having survived the Great Depression on dairy farms, she in eastern Ohio and I in eastern Pennsylvania. Dairy farming was to make great changes, but in the times we remember, a farmer with two or three dozen cows could make a decent living. Indeed, as soon as I graduated, I found work on a dairy farm.

But within a month after our wedding, Mennonite Publishing House called. Before our marriage was two months old, I had been installed as office editor for *Mennonite Community* magazine.

The pay was less than I had made on the farm where I was working, but I had considered that work only temporary. Publishing was to be long term. In a short time Mary would find work in the company bookstore, an assignment she terminated before our first son, Dennis, was born.

The preacher's daughter. We have been married for more than sixty years.

When Mary and I first met, I had no knowledge of her family or her home territory. I first met her parents when they came to Virginia for her graduation in spring 1949, and then I visited her home the following summer. I have asked myself what significance there might have been in her having been a preacher's daughter. In what ways may it have affected how we developed our life together?

I conclude that ambiguities of life in this preacher's family prepared her for marriage to a husband who overidentified with his calling as an editor and was never completely satisfied with the work he could produce. Her father, Eugene Yoder, was a farmer-preacher, a role that was common in Mennonite churches of his generation. He was expected to support himself and his family and serve the church without remuneration.

Ambiguities in her life began early, even before her father was a minister. Her life was turned upside down in 1933, when she was five years old. Her father had rented a farm in Holmes County, Ohio, the home community of her mother, Esther Miller.

For Mary, this was life in a cocoon that included her family and her sister, Martha, four years older; her church; and a community with other relatives and friendly people. Suddenly this life of security was interrupted.

The interruption came when her uncle, Willis Yoder, married and left his home in Portage County. Grandfather Rudolph determined that Mary's father as his oldest son should disband his own farm operation and come home to share with him the work on the home farm.

This called on them to move from their own house to a single-family house shared with her grandparents. They would also share the work and split the income from the dairy farm. Mary remembers the move as so upsetting that she could not stop crying until her mother took her back to the Holmes County house and showed her that other people now lived there.

For more than a dozen years, until her grandparents died in the mid-1940s, life was a delicate balance between two families.

Eventually there was a separate house for the grandparents, but yet the two family systems were joined at the hip by work and income. There were occasional celebrations such as one she remembers with pleasure: a daylong trip to the Ohio River. Yet all the time she needed to respect the wishes of the paterfamilias.

Mary was told that her grandfather had lost money in a bank that failed during the Depression. So his concern about finances was understandable. But he restricted the amount of milk the girls could drink because milk was to be sold.

Mary's mother, Esther, served as a balance wheel in this squeezed-together family system. A mild-mannered woman, she would calm her husband when he vented his frustrations. She also milked cows morning and evening. And Mary never heard her speak ill of her in-laws.

Since Martha and Mary had no brothers, they were called upon to do a boy's work as needed: Go after the cows as early as six years old, for example. Lead the horse to pull the rope that raised the hayfork from the farm wagon to the haymow. Guide the horses for the wagon that pulled a hay-loader while someone else stacked the load. And be sure to turn the corner without missing any of the hay.

When the church ordained her father, Eugene, first as a deacon and then as a preacher, there was occasional tension over time taken from the farmwork for the church. When the church called Eugene and his father saw him needed on the farm, Mary's father had to deal with the conflict.

After the grandparents died, some of the old tensions remained. Now it was necessary for Mary's father to negotiate with his siblings to settle the estate. Should he have an extra share because of the years he had spent farming with his father? Not necessarily.

By the time I arrived, Mary and her parents had moved to a smaller farm. Her father had taken his share of the cows and assembled the machinery to operate this smaller farm. But I think his heart was not in it. He had begun to drive a school bus for supplementary income.

After his wife died, he turned over the farm operation to Mary's sister, Martha, and her husband, Marcus Oswald. He moved to a house several miles away, with a large lot, a garage, and a machine shed, where he could keep a tractor and some farm equipment.

Thus enough had been happening in Mary's life that she was not surprised or upset by our move to Mennonite Publishing House. She was used to making major adjustments.

After the birth of our first son, Dennis, Mary chose homemaking and was never again to have much in the way of significant income of her own. For several years our life was to involve travel here and there while I completed work for a degree at Goshen College Biblical Seminary. But by January 1, 1957, we were able to move to our own house on a 3.46-acre lot three miles from Scottdale. Mary could now settle into her role as homemaker.

Once during the years that followed, she was offered the assignment of receptionist and telephone operator at Mennonite Publishing House. Mary declined this offer, reasoning that one absentee in the family was enough. She would support the family system from our home.

At some point I learned that Mary had once aspired to be a nurse, but her father blocked the way because nurses would work on Sunday. Of course, he himself milked cows and preached on Sunday. But since preaching was not paid, perhaps that didn't count as breaking the Sabbath.

When we learned that Mary could study at Westmoreland County Community College to become a licensed practical nurse, I suggested this to her. But she declined the offer, maintaining her position as homemaker and a volunteer in the church.

Nine times she stretched the meaning of homemaker by going to one of the homes of our three married sons to help the family at the birth of a grandchild. Our son Ronald is impressed by "the way Mom doted on the grandkids, particularly when they were small."

Our house was not finished when we moved in, but it was the kind of house she wanted—a log house. I erected it with major assistance from Ralph Hernley and Stanley Yoder. Ralph had sold us the house kit, and Stanley lived nearby. We moved in with three small boys: Dennis was three and a half years old; Ronald and Gerald, twins who had been born on Dennis's second birthday, were eighteen months old. A fourth son, Daniel Mark, was born three and a half years later.

Feeding and caring for the family on a church worker's salary called for all the creativity Mary had learned as a preacher's daughter. But as she affirmed time and again, this has been a house that she likes. As I've gone out on trips and to work, she has maintained her presence at home, providing stability that served our family well. She was executive director, chief cook, and head nurse.

Gerald recalls his mother's competence in providing food for the family:

> Caring for four hungry boys required a particular skill to prepare and serve three meals and many snacks on a $20 weekly budget. Mom was quite adept at developing casseroles to extend the food volume. Tuna noodle, chicken and rice, and ham and scalloped potatoes—these were all well received. I don't believe there were ever any leftovers. Also featured were the never-empty cookie jar and thick slices of homemade bread to ameliorate the gnawing hunger pangs associated with growth.

Dennis remembers that she was good at finding bargains, including a store in Connellsville where she could purchase ice cream for fifty-nine cents a half gallon. Gerald continues:

> In addition, raising four active boys demanded that Mom nurse children with numerous aches, pains, fevers, earaches, and fractured limbs. I think Doc Gilbert was never shocked to see us standing on the porch of his office building.

I also seem to remember that you [Dad] were absent when I broke my arm while horsing around. When making the familiar visit to the doctor's office, Mom grasped one end of my arm while Doc Gilbert grabbed the other, and they jerked my out-of-place bone back into position. I remember the pain nearly sent me to my knees. But setting the bone in his office prevented a more complicated procedure that would have been required if swelling had occurred.

My work called on me to travel at times. Two-to-four-day absences were fairly common, but two longer trips remain in my mind. In 1963 I went to Green Lake, Wisconsin, for a thirteen-day seminar on group dynamics. In 1967 I attended Mennonite World Conference in Holland and then traveled in Europe following the conference. I was gone for twenty-four days.

Mary devised a special activity to help the boys deal with my absence. As a family, we seldom took meals in restaurants, but my absences became occasions to eat out. An absence of a day or two called for a Dairy Queen visit, and a longer one suggested a complete meal. One particularly popular restaurant was the Howard Johnson in New Stanton, Pennsylvania. They had a Friday evening special with all the fish you could eat. Our sons could eat a lot of fish.

As time went on, I became aware of a whole string of practical abilities that Mary was able to develop to enhance our family life. Food-preparation skills had already been polished. She had learned these from her mother. From the beginning of our marriage, we planted a garden. Canning food came naturally, and once we could afford a food freezer, we also froze food for the winter. After I retired, we preserved the food together. Earlier she did it alone.

There were some crafts Mary had not learned at home, but now she took instruction. Braiding rugs is an example: both small rugs and large ones. The two largest are roughly nine by twelve feet and are still in use in our house, one in our bedroom and the other in the study.

Another craft involved re-covering furniture. We could buy a used sofa—which we did—and Mary could recover it for considerably less than a new one would cost. Twice she re-covered this sofa. She also re-covered furniture for our family and for friends, and even took such projects from farther afield for a fee, but never charged enough. Finally she gave up re-covering because pulling the fabric tight was too hard on her elbow.

A correspondence course in interior decorating honed her instincts in this field. Decorating the house and arranging the furniture were her prerogatives, and I seldom entered into this unless invited—except that she largely allowed me liberty in my study, which is not as tidy as she might wish.

Outside the house her artistic instincts have been expressed through flowers, both perennials and annuals. There are four permanent flower beds as well as clumps of flowers in corners here and there. Also one section of the garden down by the road is reserved for flowers and is covered with manure every other year, like the rest of the garden.

Mary majored in flowers, and I in vegetables and fruit, but we helped each other. Mary insisted that she enjoyed pulling weeds in the strawberry patch!

She also enjoyed staying at home more than traveling. Her system does not respond well to change. Sleeping in a strange bed is a challenge. But on several occasions she went along with me on extended trips. In 1975 I went as a reporter to the assembly of the World Council of Churches in Nairobi, Kenya. Mary went also, and before and after the assembly we visited Mennonite churches and activities in Africa.

The food did not always agree with her, and she lost considerable weight. But she took a set of pictures that were used to illustrate the articles I wrote for the *Gospel Herald*. In 1980 we took a sixteen-week trip around the border of the United States, visiting Mennonite congregations. From this we produced a book, *From Germantown to Steinbach*.[44]

Mary's certificate in junior college Bible was not in vain. She taught Sunday school and vacation Bible school throughout a period that would have been considered a professional career if it had been a paid activity.

Like any teacher, Mary has former students scattered throughout the country. Among them are five little girls she taught one year in Sunday school. For Christmas she made them each a little red dress.

She also pioneered in several church-related activities. Mary became the first female elder at the former Kingview Mennonite Church of Scottdale (Pa.). She was also the first female editor of Allegheny Mennonite Conference *News*, a periodical publication related to the activities of this district conference. Mary had a good camera and gave special attention to photographs for the publication.[45] In 2013 we published *The Tall Man*, a selection of editorials from the eight years she was editor.

It never occurred to me to ask how it happened that this farm girl from northeastern Ohio was found in a college library in Virginia. Ronald wondered about this and asked, "Coming from a farm family that struggled mightily, might there be something to her father's providing the means and willingness to have a daughter attend college?"

The answer is that he did not provide the means, and Mary was not sent to college. Instead, she was permitted to attend college, and she paid for it herself with money earned by cleaning houses for neighbors and by working in the laundry and the dining hall at the college.

Why did she do it? Mary went to college because it was a goal she had developed on her own. She taught the Bible to children and perceived a need for Bible training.

On reflection, she thinks it may also have been a response to the fact that both of her parents had wished for more education. Her father was not able to go to high school, and her mother did not finish grade school. But they met at the Canton (Ohio) Bible school.

It is more than sixty years since I noticed that girl in the library. We still love each other, support each other, and sometimes annoy each other. It has not always been easy. I pass over family crises that might have derailed us. But here we are, and we're grateful for what we have been able to do together.

Of course it cannot last. Nothing in this life can remain. Our future is clouded by the debilitating dementia that has afflicted Mary. In the spring of 2012 it was found necessary to place her in nursing care. I visit her every day and bring her home often. The house is empty without her in spite of its being filled with her artwork and handiwork.

Even so, we were able to celebrate our sixtieth wedding anniversary on July 7, 2012 (five days early). Children and grandchildren came together in the meeting room at the nursing home to eat cake and ice cream, tell family stories, view family pictures, and end with prayer for us. A good time was had by all.

Our house at 321 Creek Road, Scottdale, Pennsylvania.

Chapter 6

A house by the side of a country road

In the mid-1950s, when Mary and I elected to build a house in the country, we joined an urban-to-rural movement that has been prevalent in our country. I have heard that this trend is more common in Pennsylvania than in some other states. We have taken land that was once used for farming and divided it into small, family-sized plots. The three-mile road on which we live once had six or eight resident farmers. Now there are none, although some farming is still being done.

After our twins, Ronald and Gerald, were born in 1955, on the second birthday of our oldest son, Dennis, we knew we had to do something about housing. Five of us were living in four rooms on the third floor of the Mennonite Publishing House building. Having been raised on the farm, we looked for a house in the country.

Most of the prospects did not appeal to us, although there was one reasonable house at a reasonable price at a reasonable distance from town. But the building was right against the busy West Pittsburgh Street extension. We could not see submitting our impulsive small sons to this sort of temptation and danger.

So we decided to build a house. H. Ralph Hernley, production manager at Mennonite Publishing House, lived three miles from Scottdale and had bought a small farm after the owner died. He had it surveyed into large family plots. Ralph offered us 3.46 acres with 400 feet of frontage along Creek Road, which at that time was unpaved. The price, at $750, was right—unbelievable today—but it took most of our savings.

Ralph also sold us a house, a prepackaged log building similar to his house and that of his brother-in-law, Millard Lind. He even helped with construction, beginning with the excavation of the basement, using his Farmall Super C tractor. We encountered stone ledges that the Super C could not handle, so we used two cases of dynamite. But stones from the excavation later served to cover our patio.

Ralph worked for us at $1.50 an hour along with Stanley Yoder, who had recently built his own house half a mile away and worked at the same rate. Their skills made the erection possible. Others in our church community volunteered from time to time. I had built chicken coops and done rough carpenter work on the farm where I grew up, but I came to discern that building a house was a much more complex operation.

We ordered a house kit early in 1956 and began excavation in the spring. It seemed an unusually rainy year. Did it rain every day in July? When we finally got the roof on, we could work in any kind of weather.

The logs of this house were intended to be placed vertically instead of horizontally, as most log houses seem to be done. It may have been designed as a vacation home, to be set on a concrete slab with no basement. We put a basement under it, with the logs standing upright on the wall plate *beside* the floor joists.

Stanley recommended 2 × 10 floor joists to make a stiffer floor—less likely to bounce when we walked on it. We discovered that the height of the joists subtracted from the height of the ceiling. So we added 2 x 4s and 4 x 4s on top of the logs to have a higher ceiling.

s on top of the logs to have a higher ceiling. Even so, it is not much more than seven feet high. But a low ceiling saves heat.

Our house is small, 21 feet wide by 42½ feet long, with a 10 × 10 side room. This is only about 1,000 square feet, but it was what we thought we could afford. With a basement under it, we had room to raise our four sons (Dan Mark was born in 1960). By the fall of 1956, the furnace was installed and the flooring put down. As winter came on, we anticipated moving.

So on January 1, 1957, we moved to our new house. Moving on the first of the month saved us a month's rent, which I think was something less than $30. Running water was available in the bathroom, but not yet in the kitchen, although this was soon to come. It was our house—even though a lot of work was yet to be done.

One basic problem needed early attention. The dining room door faced west, with no protection from the wind. Once on the way to the doctor with one of the boys, the wind blew a $20 bill away from Mary. (Dr. Gilbert said that call would be on the house.) Something had to be done.

Mervin Swartzentruber became the next savior. He designed a garage and breezeway that would protect that door and provide a stairway to the basement. This stairway took the place of one that had cramped an already too small dining room. So in summer 1960 Mervin and I built the garage and breezeway.

Seven years later Mervin came again, and we installed two bedrooms and a bath in the basement. Now the boys could sleep in the basement.

Mary has a feel for design. At one time she was even taking a correspondence course on interior decoration. I generally left decisions on such matters to her. She braided two large rugs for use on the hardwood floor in our living room. One was braided from old coats, and the other was made from new wool.

She learned rug braiding in a course at the local YMCA. After mastering this craft, she later taught the course herself. When the floor in the living room seemed to call for refinishing, she proposed covering it with carpet. So we moved the rugs to the bedroom and the study, where they seem to be indestructible. The one made from old coats is more durable than the one made from new wool.

The two nearby log houses that were similar to ours were painted brown, so we went with red. We tried a stain, but this did not seem durable, so we settled for red paint. Mary and I would work together. I painted from the ladder, and she followed, painting what she could easily reach from the ground.

In 2009 Dennis helped with the painting. This provided more relief than we would have imagined. He also persuaded his siblings to help him buy a twenty-foot extension ladder for my birthday. It replaced the sixteen-foot ladder, which was a little too short.

Financing a house called for some creativity since most of our money had gone for the lot. Mennonite Publishing House had been financing workers' houses. I think we obtained their last mortgage: $9,000 at 4¾ percent interest. We paid it off over 17 years at $30 every two weeks, deducted from my wages.

In addition, we borrowed all we could get from the newly organized Mennonite Credit Union (from 1955). My father gave us several hundred dollars, and Mary's father loaned us $1,000. (Some years later when I decided it was time to begin repaying the loan, he sent the check back.) Laura Showalter had money to loan at 6 percent, and Paul Erb gave us $20.

How we financed the 1960 construction is not clear in my memory, but it may have been from the credit union and/or Laura Showalter. And any rate, my estimate of the total cost of the house through the 1960 addition was roughly $15,000. This was about the same as the cost of a new car we bought in 2001.

In the mid-1970s we had an unusual snowstorm on the last day of November. This very wet snow continued for only four hours, but after it ceased, we could hear tree branches breaking in the woods across the creek. Our electric power went off and was not restored for six days.

That winter I learned about heating with wood: a new type of woodstove had been developed that kept more of the heat inside instead of sending so much up the chimney. We bought one of these stoves and have used it as a supplement to our oil furnace.

We do not have a sophisticated arrangement. The woodstove is in the basement, under the duct for the cold-air return to the furnace. We cut a hole in the duct, and when the furnace fan turns on, it draws heat from the stove into the system. All I can say about the relative efficiency is that the first year we used the woodstove, it cut our oil consumption in half.

The woodstove keeps the basement warm and generally makes the atmosphere of the house more cheerful in winter. But like the fossil fuels—coal, oil, and gas—heating with wood is only a stopgap strategy until we are able to use heat from the sun more directly.

Some years ago people were asking how soon we would move to a retirement center. I do not seem to have heard that challenge recently. Maybe they have given up on this notion for us. As long as I can keep up with the house, the garden, and a lawn, why not do it?

Recently it occurred to me that Polly and Jim Cutrell have the only other household that was present in this small community at the time we built our house. Our neighborhood has changed. Yet when the Savanick house next to us was sold to David and Barbara Lynn, we found them to be friendly neighbors. In more than a dozen years side by side, we have had no conflicts and on occasion have been able to do favors for each other.

We are comfortable in our house beside a country road. Yet we are aware that ours is not an energy-efficient strategy. Like many Americans, we have too large a lawn, which in the English custom calls for regular mowing with a gasoline-powered mower. I saw an old-fashioned reel mower at the hardware store and was tempted but not quite ready to go back to that. And I recently bought a riding mower.

All the services we need are somewhere else. In recent years full-service grocery stores have migrated farther away. We do not have clear answers to questions about the waste of energy. To be more energy efficient, people need to live in a town where they can walk for basic services and have access to public transportation. Those of us living in the country are prisoners of the automobile system.

What was expected to deliver country people from isolation and make transportation more convenient and pleasurable—this motoring has become a burden, weighing us down. It appears that this system is so entrenched that a solution to the problem will not be found in our time or in that of our children. Maybe our grandchildren can help to solve it for the good of the planet and the continuation of human life. (See chapter 9 below.)

Chapter 7

Gardening 101

It was to be expected that Mary and I would plant a garden. We never asked the question. We just planted a garden at the first opportunity. We both grew up on farms where there were gardens. As a boy I had worked in a garden under duress, but I had learned some things about how to do it.

When we moved to Scottdale, we learned that a garden plot was available for rent. A farmer would plow and disk the lot, and we would take it from there.

One memory of this early Scottdale garden is that in summer 1953 I went away for a week to a writers' conference. Mary was eight months pregnant, and on the way to the garden she slipped into a hole and scraped her leg on a stone. The scar is with her yet.

Nevertheless in 1954, when we moved to Goshen, Indiana, for me to attend seminary, we had several dozen glass jars of canned goods for use during the winter.

Since we moved to the country, we have always planted a garden. Does it pay to raise our own food in a garden, or should we allow the large-scale mechanized farms and food factories to supply it? This payback question we have never seriously entertained. We do not keep careful records of our garden or other food costs.

I have noticed, however, that the price of the garden seeds we order once a year by mail is roughly similar to the cost of groceries we generally purchase for a two-week period. But that is only a rough comparison. We buy tomato and cabbage plants and seed potatoes locally. Various other expenses boost the cost.

I think this was a year when the foliage was abundant but there were no lima beans.

In his book *The $64 Tomato*, William Alexander reports his and his wife's conclusion:

> The gardening is worth it, in the first place for the food. . . . There is really nothing like a fresh August tomato. . . . Gardening is by its very nature an expression of the triumph of optimism over experience. No matter how bad this year was, there's always next year.[46]

I reviewed this book the year we spent $350 for reconstructive surgery on our garden tiller. However, I found that Alexander put money into things we get along nicely without, such as paying someone to design the garden before gardening even began.

As our gardening instincts matured, we found that Mary would major in flowers, I would emphasize vegetables and fruits (anything edible), and we would help each other. I have never quite comprehended how it is that Mary insisted she enjoyed pulling weeds. But it is one activity where you can readily observe the results of your work. In return, I have sprayed her roses with Liquid Fence to keep the deer away.

Mary's flower gardens are extensive, and her flowers have come from a variety of sources. Most of the roses are from Jackson and Perkins in Oregon, but some can be traced to Grandma Miller in Holmes County, Ohio. Some of the primroses come from there also, but others are from seed we bought at Butchart Gardens in British Columbia, near Victoria.

A list of Mary's perennials appears as Appendix B (below). Notable among these are peonies, of course, and iris as well, yet also red hot poker, coral bells, clematis, and butterfly plants. Brown-eyed Susans and various lilies need to be thinned on occasion to keep them from taking over the flower beds. Dahlia tubers are dug in the fall and stored inside to keep them from freezing.

Gardening is a year-round preoccupation. Indeed, I have seen ads for a solar greenhouse, which would permit me to grow salad greens all winter long. I considered this but concluded that I need a break in the winter. Better to think about gardening for a couple of months and then begin again with enthusiasm.

If I plant lettuce at the right time, cover it, and keep the slugs at bay, we can eat our own lettuce into December. Soon after Christmas the seed catalogs begin to arrive. So then is the time to think about gardening and review the gardening books on the shelf while resisting Rodale's offer of another book. By late February or early March (depending on the season), gardening begins.

First to be planted are lettuce, spinach, and radishes. Indeed, if I have done the right thing in the fall and the winter is not too severe, there may be overwintered spinach ready even earlier than the new produce. In any case I cover the early plantings with a row cover, which lets in the sun and rain but keeps off the frost.

Then with a wider window of opportunity come peas and carrots, reasonably frost tolerant. After the danger of frost is waning, all the rest of the garden crowd may be planted. Almost half of the yearly garden space goes for sweet corn, with several different varieties. Differing maturation dates and planting at different times extend the season of fresh corn.

Our gardening efforts have been aided and abetted through by-products of a local dairy operation. Since corn is a heavy feeder, the manure is applied during the corn year, with the assumption that the crops that follow in rotation the next year will profit from the leftovers. Ours is not a strictly organic garden, but basically so.

It has been claimed that healthy crops are of less interest to insects. Indeed, I have not seen a Mexican bean beetle for years. However, corn earworms seem not to have gotten the message. With considerable hesitation, I assault them with carbaryl.

With the usually bulging food freezer, we seldom buy canned or frozen vegetables. Better to eat those from our own garden. At times we do indulge in celery, one crop that calls for more special handling than we care to apply. We also buy lettuce and occasionally cabbage when ours are out of season.

And our stored carrots do not last until the new crop is ready.

Each gardening season is different. It is as if the gardener plays ping-pong with the weather. Will there be enough rain or too much rain? A late frost in the spring or an early frost in the fall? Which crop will do better with which weather? Most garden crops profit from regular showers. Corn especially needs some rain when the ears are forming. What my father used to call a "corn shower" may be a quarter of an inch of rain or maybe even less, but it needs to come at the right time.

Of even more concern than the weather are the contests with insects and varmints, the famous triumvirate of rabbits, woodchucks, and raccoons. Also at times, possums. Each calls for vigilance and an appropriate response. Cabbage worms, for example, will invade the broccoli heads, but a specific insecticide called BT strikes them down. As for the triumvirate, each calls for a different tactic.

For rabbits, there is Liquid Fence, intended to keep away both deer and rabbits. It seems to work for deer, but for rabbits the results are inconclusive. The raccoons will have sweet corn, and the woodchucks will have a number of things, particularly carrot tops. They do not seem to be attracted to the vines of the nightshade family such as tomatoes and potatoes. But I prefer my own carrots and like to grow broccoli and cabbage, which woodchucks seem to consider delectable.

I have used two tactics with raccoons: trap and haul away, or put an electric fence around the corn. Neither one seems completely effective. I haul the trapped coons three miles away to a place where there are no nearby gardens. Some say they will come back. Ever on guard, I also put up an electric fence around the corn. I dare not get careless with the fence, or the coons will find a way into the corn.

Woodchucks are another issue. I have caught some in the trap by using apples as bait. But a fence that will stop a rabbit will not stop a woodchuck, which just goes under it. This is a fight to the death: you shoot or trap the woodchuck or put smoke bombs in their holes.

I've done all three, but the problem with the first is to see the animal and then be able to aim straight. The smoke works if you find the burrow. But in some years there seems to be an endless supply of new woodchucks moving into the holes

At times I may wonder with William Alexander whether saving our carrot tops from woodchucks is worth all the effort. Then I remember that I can eat the carrots from my own garden ten months of the year, and I do not cherish the woody texture of those from the grocery store.

Of course an abundance of food is available for a price. Too many in our society are hungry, but there are plenty of resources if our own program fails. Gardening 101 is basic food production. One reason to live in the country is to be able to have space for a garden. However, some in the cities are also beginning to plant gardens.

Yet as I drive along our country roads, I'm disappointed to see that many are not planting gardens. Why not? Maybe they think they don't have time. Maybe they think it doesn't pay. Maybe they've never learned how. Basic skills for food production have not been passed on to them. Who will instruct them?

Some are willing to forego gardening to have a better view of wild life. In *Appalachian Spring*, Marcia Bonta writes about life on their 500-acre farm on the edge of Laurel Ridge in southwestern Pennsylvania. She and her family have decided in favor of wild life. "We have had to resign ourselves to the natural look in landscaping, growing only those flowers, herbs, and vegetables the wild animals don't like."[47] For me, this would be a major adjustment.

There is no typical year in gardening. As I have said, we play ping-pong with the weather and must be ever vigilant against the forays of the insects and varmints. The year 2009 was a remarkable gardening year for us. The season did not begin as early as some (March instead of February), but early plants came on apace.

The peas were planted at a good time, and plenty of rain in May pushed them along. A woodchuck clipped some, but results were rather good except that some of the vines lodged because of ample rain, and some of the peas rotted from excess moisture. Maybe I should put up a fence for them next year. I've never been inclined to go to that extra effort.

The peach trees did not bloom at all, but the apples needed to be thinned, and the strawberries came through well. The new variety of red lettuce given to us by Jim Cutrell grew and regrew until the end of July. The green beans outdid themselves. Most of the early corn got rain just in time for pollination, but somehow raccoons got in and raided the patch. Either the electric fence was not turned on or something wasn't working.

A woodchuck stripped the soybeans and convinced me to stop raising them. Keeping varmints away from the soybeans seemed to be just too much trouble. (Then in 2012 I found myself ordering soybean seed again.)

Also, blight hit the tomatoes. I read about it in the paper, but before I learned what to spray, it was too late for a dozen plants. As instructed, I pulled them, put them in plastic bags, and sent them to the landfill. This was the first year we encountered tomato blight. The year before we had so many tomatoes we gave some away. In 2009 we had to buy them if we wanted to can tomato juice.

Potatoes looked hopeful. Even if they might have been blighted, they still had potatoes underground. The blight destroys the tomato fruit.

So gardening is not for the faint of heart. But I tell myself over and over that I prefer my own carrots instead of the woody ones found in the grocery store. If I can stop the coons, I have sweet corn direct from the garden. And that cannot be beat.

The bees on the left side are loafing. There may be a shortage of nectar bearing flowers. The colony on the right is weak and is being fed sugar water.

Chapter 8

A beekeeper must pay attention

In times too far back to remember, numbers of wild creatures have been domesticated: cattle, for example, sheep, goats. Dogs, I once read, were not domesticated. They just began hanging around.

Honeybees have never been domesticated. Their relationship to humans is a marriage of convenience. If we provide a place for them and they find it satisfactory, they will move in. If not satisfactory, they move on. They are not here to do our bidding. Yet over some thousands of years, people have been manipulating the bees, and so much the more in modern times.

I should never have become a beekeeper. A beekeeper should be the kind of person I am not: deliberate, careful, precise. I have seen persons working with bees while wearing a T-shirt. I did it myself once with bees from a package. I was most impressed by their gentleness, but I eventually learned that package bees are young bees, and when they get older, they become more crotchety.

Yet by selective breeding it has been possible to develop bees that will put up with the beekeeper's manipulations as long as these are done slowly and methodically.

The memory of how I first began working with bees is not very clear. My brother Truman remembers that we started with a swarm. I suppose we got some honey from them, but my clearest memory is that I found I could tolerate multiple stings. That is an important qualification for beekeepers, particularly those with a large number of hives. In a day's work they will probably encounter some bees that are less gentle, and so they will endure occasional stings.

I have protective clothing, and I usually wear it: nylon coveralls with a veil attached by a zipper. When the zipper is closed, bees can buzz me without being able to sting. But on occasion a bee will get up my pants leg or inside a glove.

If I open a hive and the bees become disturbed in spite of the use of the smoker, more than a dozen may buzz me. If so, I generally take a walk, sometimes through the woods, and eventually most of them will give up and go back to the hive.

On occasion I have heard "the birds and the bees" suggested as examples for the sex education of children. The birds perhaps fit, but I cannot see how the sexuality of bees connects at all with human sexuality. The sexuality of bees is specialized and strictly functional. There is no romance.

There are three classes of honeybees: workers, queens, and drones (the male bees). Most abundant are the workers, labeled as incomplete females. They are in charge of the hive. The workers live to work, to build up the colony, and to protect the hive. If a queen is lost, some of the workers may become laying workers, but this is a desperate last stand. All that can hatch from their eggs are drones, and the colony will die since drones are not able to work.

A colony that is healthy has a queen. The queen does not rule the colony. Her function is to lay eggs, and the workers provide space for her. In one sense she is in charge: her pheromone, or odor, permeates the hive. As long as her odor is strong, the colony is content. When she grows old and the odor is no longer strong, the workers know it is time to raise a new queen.

Before a new queen emerges, the colony will probably swarm. A sizable number of the bees conduct the old queen out of the hive and look for a new place. They first cluster nearby and send out scouts to look for a suitable place. If the beekeepers are alert, they may put a hive under the cluster and shake down the bees. If the hive is satisfactory, they will ignore the scouts when they come back and settle down.

In the meantime, one or more new queens will appear and take a mating flight. Here is where the drones become important. A drone cannot work or feed himself. His function is to have sex once in his life. His body breaks apart in the act of copulation, but he has made his contribution to the ongoing life of the bees.

This all happens in the air. The queen may receive semen from more than one drone and may make more than one mating flight. In any case, she will receive enough semen to fertilize all of the eggs she will lay during the rest of her life.

A colony of bees operates on the assumption that there will never be quite enough honey, so they try to supply a surplus. A worker bee will live a month or six weeks in the busy season, going through a series of tasks, first in the hive and finally out in the field, bringing in its lifetime enough nectar to make 1/12 teaspoon of honey. The beekeeper profits from the bees' penchant for abundance. When the colony is in good shape, they will store more honey then they will ever need, and the beekeeper will share in the largesse.

Beekeeping as done today depends on the work of L. L. Langstroth, a nineteenth-century beekeeper with a better-than-average facility for observation. He noticed the "bee space," the space the bees leave in between their combs. So he began to provide wooden frames for their combs. The frames could then be lifted out of the hive to examine the state of the colony. Modern beekeeping has developed from this innovation.

Today some beekeepers own thousands of colonies and transport them from place to place for nectar and pollination. It is reported that the value of pollination is more important for the economy than the value of the honey. Almond production in California depends on bees brought in from as far away as West Virginia.

At one point Mary was ready to help me with beekeeping, but we discovered that she is allergic to bee venom, so she had to give it up. However, she was still willing to "hive" a swarm if I was out of town, which sometimes happened when I was an editor. Swarming bees are less likely to sting because they have no hive to protect.

On one occasion she was summoned to a swarm in Scottdale. As she has reported, when she arrived, she found the swarm on a grapevine a few feet off the ground. A crowd had gathered, and a policeman kept saying, "Stand back." One old lady said, "I'll pray for you."

Mary put on protective clothing and put a hive under the bees. She shook the vine, and as soon as the bees dropped to the ground, they began to enter the hive. Everyone was most impressed.

A beekeeper must pay attention. Following Langstroth's example, we can open a hive and examine the state of the colony, and we need to do this from time to time. One thing we need to know is whether the colony has a good queen.

It is not necessary to see the queen if we see the results of her work. The results will appear as eggs in cells, larvae in unsealed cells, and pupae in sealed cells. The brood pattern should be regular, not scattered, with large phalanxes of sealed brood ready to hatch and go to work.

If the queen is no longer satisfactory, she should be replaced. Some say we should do this routinely every year or two anyway. To replace a queen, you need to find her and kill her. Then you insert a new queen in the hive with sugar candy in the opening of her cage. The theory is that after the bees have spent several days cleaning out this candy, they are more likely to accept the new queen.

I have requeened hives, but it is a delicate operation. When you want to find the old queen, she is likely hiding, and it may take special efforts to find her. The alternative to requeening is to let the bees take care of the succession. Then they may swarm, and if the beekeeper is present, the swarm can be captured. But if not, the swarm will probably go over the hills and far away.

After more than forty years of beekeeping, I know a few basic things about it. One of these is that I can never be entirely sure what the bees will do or what will happen to them. Every spring I check the hives to see whether the colonies have lived through the winter. To have them all survive is a beekeeper's victory.

Like all living organisms, bees have afflictions. One of the recent problems has been varroa mites. This insect is about as big as a pinhead. It likes to lay eggs in the cells of the larvae. When the mites flourish, the colony will probably die.

We have fought back against varroa with various means. First we used chemicals, but in addition to the danger to the bees and perhaps to us, the mites tended to become resistant. More recently we have used organic substances such as formic acid. But in the long run it appears that if there is to be success, it will be in developing strains of bees that can fight back at the mites.

Certain suppliers of bees have deliberately not treated their bees and just perpetuated those that survived. It may be that some bees are developing resistance on their own. After several years when there seemed to be few if any swarms, there have been some swarms recently. Where the swarms come from, we often do not know, but it seems that some are coming from holes in trees or openings in buildings and have been living on their own.

More recently another affliction turned up that has been labeled "colony collapse disorder." All the mature bees disappear, and a colony may be left with a queen, a few young bees, and plenty of honey. As of this writing, the source of the problem is not completely clear: insecticides? viruses? Some have suggested various combinations of causes.

I wonder whether transporting bees thousands of miles may make them more vulnerable. When in a recent spring I found that all my colonies had survived the winter, I was reassured but not completely comfortable.

When the problems of bees seemed almost too much to bear, I have considered giving up on beekeeping. Indeed, I would not feel right without some bees around, particularly on the peach and apple trees. To see a bee on a blossom is somehow reassuring. There is plenty wrong in the world, but one system is still functioning: bees are pollinating and making honey. And I hardly ever meet a honeybee I don't like.

In mid-March 2012 the thought came to me that I should stop beekeeping. Mary needed more help than I could give while still caring for the bees. The bees had to go.

Chapter 9

Transportation follies

As of this writing, I have held title to fourteen cars and two pickup trucks over a period of some sixty years. Whether this is a boast or a confession depends on whether one views the automobile as a technological victory or an ecological disaster.

I was born in the middle of the 1920s, a U.S. automobile decade, near the end of the Model T Ford era. Henry Ford had built a car that sold at a price low enough for his own employees to buy one, along with large numbers of other ordinary Americans.

But in December 1927 the Ford Motor Company brought out the new Model A. This event is explained by Frederick Lewis Allen:

> Model T had been losing to Chevrolet its leadership of the enormous low-priced-car market, for the time had come when people were no longer content with ugliness and a maximum speed of forty or forty-five miles an hour; no longer content, either, to roar slowly uphill with the weary left foot jammed against a low-speed pedal while robin's-egg-blue Chevrolets swept past in second [gear].

Allen reports that the appearance of the Model A was a major event. "For weeks and months, every new Ford that appeared on the streets drew a crowd."[48]

My father was in no position to buy one of the new Fords. In the several years after I was born, I was joined by two sisters and two brothers. Dad had to support this growing family, and

The van: it was not very comfortable but each boy could have his own window.

the farm income was shared with his mother, who owned the farm, and his brother Milford, who was a partner. In the early 1930s the brothers bought a 1925 two-door Dodge sedan for use as a farm truck. On Sunday Dad would put the seats back in the car, and we would go to church in it. We had one of the oldest cars in the churchyard.

My first car, bought for $1,125 cash in 1947, when I was twenty-one, was a 1941 Dodge that had survived the war years. I bought it with the understanding that my younger brother Truman would take it over when I left for college in the fall. It was a bad investment, but Truman was more impacted than I. It got us into the automobile system, where we have been ever since.

As Allen observes, the automobile "changed the face of America. Towns which had once been prosperous because of proximity to a railroad lost out if the highway passed them by. Trolleys eventually gave it up, and railroads had to adjust."[49] So today we're stuck with the automobile, especially if we do not live in a city with adequate public transportation.

In *Autophobia*, Brian Ladd writes, "Once we have cars—and especially once there are nearly as many cars as drivers—we can fully benefit from the great convenience they offer. Yet as we organize our lives around their needs, the freedom they bring can begin to feel more like slavery."[50]

For more than sixty-five years I have been freed by automobiles and have accepted the accompanying slavery. Access to autos has freed Mary and me to live three miles from town without public transportation. It has made it possible for us to pursue goods and services as they left our small town, no doubt in part because of the freeing impact of automobiles and trucks.

We have been freed to replace these cars from time to time, not always wisely or well, but we did what we could. Our four sons learned to drive with the advantage of driving instruction in school, and all passed the Pennsylvania driving tests. So now they also have accepted the freedom and slavery of automobile ownership.

A part of the slavery assumed with the purchase of an automobile is the responsibility to keep it repaired. Like any mechanical device, it is subject to decay. At times it will require repairs, especially if the owner is able to afford only a used car. On occasion, when the cost of keeping my teeth repaired seems high, I reflect on the high price of repairing an auto.

Because I owned it for only a short time, the 1941 Dodge never quite became my own car. So the other thirteen remain in memory, each of them distinctive in its own way, some more than others.

In December 1948 I bought a second car for $100, a 1930 Marquette. This served as my personal transportation for three and a half years and provided some remarkable adventures in repairing its problems. The Marquette, according to its story in *Wikipedia*, was produced for only one year, 1930.

It was intended to be a lower-priced alternative to Buick and sold quite well. But "Buick executives didn't feel that enough Marquettes were sold to warrant the extra burden on the bottom line given the state of the economy." So my Marquette at its age of eighteen years was bound to be distinctive, both as a novelty and by the nature of its problems.

The problems causing the most extensive distress were the tailpipe and fuel-pump scenario. First, the tailpipe. At its age I was not surprised that the tailpipe needed to be replaced, but obviously I would not get a new one off the rack at Pep Boys. I should have arranged for a welder to produce a customized tailpipe, but that seemed too expensive.

I heard about a flexible tailpipe, although these were not legal in Pennsylvania. So I changed registration of the car to Virginia, where it was legal, and thought the problem was solved.

It was not that simple: in the meantime the fuel pump went out of business. Someone suggested an electric fuel pump. All right. We hooked it up to the heater switch and were on our way. Yet one day on a trip to Ohio, the car kept choking down. The problem was finally identified as vapor lock. The flexible tailpipe had broken off, and the stub was pointing directly at the gas tank, preheating the gas and causing vapor lock.

Vapor lock pursued me as long as I used the electric fuel pump. On a cool morning the car would run well. On a warm afternoon it was continually choking down. No new fuel pump was available. The problem was finally solved when a mechanic rebuilt the old fuel pump. "It ought to work now," he said. "It's got all new guts."

When I was graduating from college and expecting to be married, I looked for better wheels. I passed up the chance to buy a well-maintained 1937 Chevrolet (15 years old) and bought a 1942 Studebaker "with a '47 motor." (Bad idea!) The Studebaker was succeeded by a 1947 Plymouth in which the piston rings had been replaced. (Good value.) This was followed by 1949 Plymouth, a well-designed auto, but by the time we got it, the engine was into automotive dementia.

Next came a seven-year-old 1953 two-door Chevrolet with only 30,000 miles at the bargain price of $300. It served for four years and 50,000 miles yet had a few quirks related to its two-speed Powerglide transmission. On a level road it would perform well enough, but on our western Pennsylvania hills, it was continually shifting between low and high. The "lugging" in high was hard on the valves, and I believe I had them ground twice in four years.

This car was retired because four growing boys became too much for it to hold. We replaced it with a 1961 Chevrolet sedan (not a good choice), followed by a 1964 Chevrolet van. The main advantage of this van was that everyone could have a window. There were several disadvantages, particularly that the heater kept only the driver warm.

After the boys left home and we saw no need for a full-sized sedan, we began to buy subcompact cars: A 1972 Dodge Colt in 1976, and in 1979 our first new car, a Mazda GLC. The Mazda had a 1.4 liter four-cylinder engine and never broke any speed records. But it lasted nine years and 130,000 miles.

Its place was taken by a Mercury Tracer. Like the '42 Studebaker and the '61 Chevy, it came to stand out among our less successful automotive purchases. I read *Consumers Reports* and found that the Tracer had a Mazda engine and that its repair record was "average." We had been well impressed by the Mazda engine, so we went with the Tracer. It was a snappy car, easy to drive, and we both liked the way it handled.

Eventually we were reminded that there is much more to a car than the engine. Other things can go wrong. I calculated that in one year the Tracer spent thirty days in a repair shop. If we had it today, I would be calling 1-800-MyLemon.

First was the two-cylinder problem. Especially on a frosty morning, the car would run for a time on only two cylinders. This was finally traced to a crack in the wire that controlled two of the fuel injectors. Well, all right. That problem was taken care of.

Then came the rear-window scenario. The Tracer had a hatchback instead of a trunk, and three different times the glass in the rear window shattered spontaneously. I never found the source of this, but I wondered if the hatch may have been slightly twisted in manufacturing. Adding to the litany of repair problems was the fuel pump and a rear wheel bearing.

The Tracer went out with a bang. At a sharp curve on a two-lane road, we were hit head-on by a young driver in a Chevrolet Celebrity (a slightly larger car). A policeman told me that this driver had pushed us nineteen feet. Mary had seatbelt burn across her chest and a broken arm. The rescue squad had to cut me out of the car, but my injuries were less extensive than hers. The Tracer was totaled.

After such a string of problems, we did not have the courage to buy another Tracer. We settled on a 1992 Honda Civic, which was followed nine and a half years later by a 2002 Honda Civic. We found the cars to be reliable if unexciting. When in 2009 we replaced the second Honda with a 2006 Toyota, I expected that the mileage would not be as good. The 1992 could get mileage in the mid-40s per gallon of gas, and the 2002 in the low 40s, but now the Toyota put us back into the 30-some miles per gallon.

Brian Ladd's *Autophobia* is subtitled *Love and Hate in the Automotive Age*. He describes the views of enthusiasts and detractors from the beginning of automobiles to the present. Ladd points out that the auto has been able to outrun or overrun all of its detractors. At the end he concludes that the advantages of the car make debatable sense:

> It makes sense if we believe that our increasingly car-centered lives are the lives we want. It makes sense if we can agree that the dark side of automobility is a price worth paying for those blessings. But we have never agreed about these matters, and we never will.[51]

As I mentioned above, Mary and I have responded to the auto dilemma by choosing smaller cars after our sons moved away. They cost less to purchase and return better mileage. However, numbers of our peers do not agree with us. We often find that ours is among the apparent minority of smaller cars in a churchyard.

In the meantime the threat of global warming troubles scientists and others. Some are seeking to develop alternatives to the internal combustion engine. I do not expect the baneful results of global warming to come soon enough to affect me very much, but if life is to go on, as I hope it will, something must be done. I think I am trying to live responsibly, but I have not been ready to stop driving and restrict myself to walking. In that sense I am part of the dilemma.

In "The Myth of the Efficient Car" (*The Progressive*, May 2009), Alex Dubro asserts that "the looming catastrophe of global pollution, including climate change, will never be solved by building more cars—efficient or otherwise." The automobile and the infrastructure required for its use are by their very nature inefficient and environmentally wasteful.

"The essence of the problem is that cars don't move people, cars move cars." A proposed 100-miles-per-gallon hypercar would not be a solution. "Even if everything is paper thin—something the public won't easily warm to—you're still driving five times your body weight around."

As for the infrastructure, the production of materials for roads and bridges—especially concrete—contributes mightily to global warming. And rubber tires on asphalt roads cause much more friction than steel on steel, as with a railcar. "The personal automobile must be abandoned and quickly."[52]

We have joined our fellow Americans in the failing automotive experiment. The ultimate price, it appears, is yet to be paid.

Chapter 10

As I was saying

From 2000 to 2007 I wrote a monthly column for the Connellsville (Pa.) *Daily Courier*. The newspaper gave permission for the reprint of these columns if I reported the date when they first appeared. My notes showed that "Canning peaches" appeared in the *Courier* on September 26, 2002; and "The death of our dog, Hund" on October 12, 2002 (before the Iraq War). I had failed to date the clipping of "My father-in-law's shovel," but research in the Carnegie Library of Connellsville indicates that it probably appeared on September 29, 2001.

Canning peaches: An art and a science

I married a wife who knew how to can peaches. She learned it from her mother. I never thought to ask about this before we married. When you are young and in love, you don't ask such questions. If ours were a culture where marriages would be negotiated by families, such a question might arise.

The father of the groom asks, "Is she able to can peaches?"

"Well no, I guess not," admits the father of the bride.

"She had better learn."

I won that one without really trying. For all the years of our married life—with only a few exceptions—my wife has canned peaches. There is an art and a science to canning peaches, but mainly a science. If you don't do it right, you won't have canned peaches.

How do you can peaches? This is a report of the process as observed with participation. It is not considered a lesson. For this you may want to contact the Agricultural Extension Office. Or ask your mother. But here is a rundown of how I saw it happen.

It is preferable to begin with good peaches. To obtain these, we may need to do some research. Since we do not live in a good fruit-growing area (too many late frosts), we will probably need to look farther away. My wife and I have had peaches from our own trees on occasion, but the trees we have now are young, and this year all the blossoms froze.

So anyhow, where will we get peaches? Chambersburg peaches are the most advertised around here. We agree that Chambersburg has good peaches, especially if we can stop on the way home from somewhere and buy them at the orchard.

Several years ago we bought Belleville peaches, and they were good also. This year someone told us about Fishertown peaches. Well, why not? We were going to a family reunion, and Fishertown was on the way. So we stopped for Fishertown peaches, and they were good.

Now we are ready to can the peaches, but first we must wait until they soften. Not too long, or they get too soft. Next begins the canning routine—an assembly line operation. One person can do it alone, as my wife has done many times, but it goes better with two.

First, bring out the fruit jars, wash them, and set them aside. Glass jars are amazing. I hope the person who invented them was reasonably rewarded. As long as they don't break or get the tops chipped, you can use them indefinitely. My wife got some of hers from her mother. Widemouthed jars work better for peaches, especially large Fishertown peaches.

Now the process begins: Heat water to boiling in a large kettle. Put eight peaches in a sack—a mesh sack we got with oranges in it—and immerse for a minute in the boiling water. Then quickly transfer the peaches to cold water. The point is to loosen the skins so they will peel easily.

Now peel them, cut each in two, and pack the halves into jars. Fill the jars, but not too full or they may run over. Drench them with sugar water and close the rings tightly over the wide-mouthed jar lids, from our favorite grocery.

Next, it gets even more scientific. Put six jars in the pressure cooker (seven if we can squeeze in another one), heat the pressure up to five pounds and hold it there for eight minutes. This is live steam, so we watch it carefully.

Then let the cooker cool down, take out the jars, and set them apart from each other to cool and seal. When the lid goes "pop," it has sealed. Let them continue to cool overnight or even longer, remove the reusable rings, and store the peaches.

That's about it for canning peaches. Except, of course, eating them, one jar at a time throughout the year—or two when we have guests for dinner. As of this writing, we have six quarts of last year's Chambersburg peaches, and we will eat them first. Then on to the Fishertown peaches.

I recommend that if it all possible you marry a wife who knows how to can peaches. You can thank her all winter long.

The death of our dog, Hund

Our dog Hund died the third week in September. We could see that he was failing throughout the summer. His winter coat did not shed properly, and his hearing waned. But he was still full of ginger at the beginning of a walk.

I had replaced his cable within the year. He tore the one before it, so I went to our favorite hardware store and bought a Cider Mill twenty-foot "tie out," the one with a St. Bernard on the package and 4,200-pound cable strength. That one outlasted him. I will keep it a while as a souvenir and then perhaps donate it to the World's Attic used-article shop in Somerset.

As I wrote in February 2001, Hund was an independent dog who had his own agenda. He had been our son's dog, but since in recent years our son has been living in places where dogs are not welcome, he became our charge. I considered it my responsibility to take him for a walk once a day.

Once when I was away from home, my wife went out with him. He saw a cat and ran after it. My wife fell down and was dragged along, hanging to the leash. She never took him for a walk again.

His final decline came so suddenly as to be a shock. On a Sunday afternoon I took him for the usual walk. Though eager to go, he did not display his usual vigor. Whereas the regular pattern was to have him ahead, urging me on, toward the end of this walk it was rather the other way around. I left that evening for several days, and my wife observed that he appeared to have a seizure.

By Tuesday evening, I cut the walk short and called our son to inform him that the dog was failing. He did not want to believe it, but he came on Thursday and saw the symptoms for himself. It was as if Hund's nervous system was closing down. Our son agreed that we had to let him go and offered to dig the grave.

After the death, my wife and I were both amazed to see how much this dog had become a part of our lives. Even though caring for him was sometimes a burden and his occasional escapes an annoyance, it was habitual for us to glance at his spot under the tree to see whether he was there.

We recall with a mixture of sadness and relief how Hund used to complain when anybody came out of the house, implying that he should be given a walk. Now I walk alone. One thing we can say: Cats and woodchucks will be safer.

Hund's fourteen years made up a significant block of time in our own lives. We're not the same people we were when he came to us. On the one hand, the stream of life is continuous, flowing like a river. But there are riffles, interruptions in the stream that make differences. Family life changes. Grandchildren are born. Others go off to college. We ourselves travel here and there. During this one dog's life, I made five trips out of the country.

If we had not had seatbelts, my wife and I might have preceded our dog by ten years—when we met a car head-on at a sharp bend near Laurelville. The other driver was evidently not familiar with the road and went too fast to stay in his lane at the sharp corner. A cop later told me that the auto had pushed our car nineteen feet. My wife carries a plate in her left arm as a memento of that accident.

The death of our dog is a reminder that life is precious. It should be received and lived joyfully, with gratitude to God. We do well to keep our relations with God and our fellow humans in good repair. We cannot be sure when our time will come. What a pity to pass from this life with either of these relationships out of order.

Our community has changed in fourteen years. Stores have closed. Others have opened. Many cars have gotten larger. Traffic has increased. Roads are repaired. Some bridges are repaired and opened again. Others remain closed, such as one near us. Because of this, I need to drive five miles to contact my friend, the Fayette County farmer. With that bridge, a mile and a half would do it.

The world has changed in fourteen years. There have been floods, tornadoes, hurricanes, earthquakes, wars and rumors of wars. The Persian Gulf War was notable. So also the September 11, 2001 attack on the World Trade Center. But there are various other wars and conflicts too numerous to mention. Today there are threats of war. We should oppose war—any war—every chance we get.

Some of the people calling the loudest for war have never been in a war. Wars are not good for living things, especially children. To resort to war shows a lack of imagination. There are better ways to resolve conflicts. We should support them.

A friend has offered us a dog, but we will pass for now. We want to be free from the obligation. And we hesitate to make the emotional commitment so soon after our bond with Hund was broken.

My father-in-law's shovel

When my father-in-law died more than twenty years ago, we inherited some rather good hand tools. Among them are a pick and mattock that share the same interchangeable handle, a scythe, a manure fork, a square short-handled shovel, a digging bar made from a reclaimed automobile axle, a posthole digger, and a regular shovel.

For twenty years I had gotten by without a bar and a posthole digger. After I had them, I wondered how I managed to get by. On a place like ours, there come occasions when I need to dig holes—such as after vandals have knocked down the mailbox, which happens every year or two. The last time they pushed down the post altogether. To replace it, I found a sturdy locust post, but it was too short. So I found a longer one and planted them both.

Now the mail carrier uses the shorter one as a place to park packages that are too large for the mailbox. The next time the vandals decide to take out our mailbox, they will encounter *two* locust posts. These may not stop them, but I consider it important to make their effort worthwhile.

Sometime ago I mislaid the digging bar. One day I went to get it from its usual place, and it was not there. Who could have it? Not my son the handyman. He affirmed that he had not borrowed it.

So I bought a new one for $29.95 at my favorite hardware store. It is sharper, longer, and has a knob at the end of the handle, but it is not as stiff as the old car axle, and I can imagine it bending in a hard pry.

Several months later I found the old bar lying in the grass. I had used it to punch a hole for a stake to protect a small tree, then forgot to put it away. Now I have two bars, but the old axle is still my favorite. It is not as sharp, not as tall, and there's no knob on the end, but I trust it more.

I do trust my father-in-law's shovel. There is nothing fancy about it. The identification is straightforward and unpretentious: "Heat Treated Woods 2 Light Weight."

There are two other shovels in the garage. Both are also "Heat Treated," and both have longer blades, although one has no handle. I seldom use them. I have no need to as long as I have my father-in-law's shovel; its blade is shorter, but it stays sharp.

Sharp enough to cut the smaller roots I sometimes encounter while digging a hole.

I can imagine the time might come when I'm careless and break the handle. But I try to be careful. I would like to be able to use the shovel another twenty years and perhaps then pass it on to my son the handyman.

The purpose of a shovel, of course, is to be able to dig a hole or shovel dirt as needed. For this any shovel will do. But I find it somehow reassuring that I have been able use my father-in-law's shovel for more than twenty years. It has already outlived one computer, several automobiles, a toaster, a vacuum cleaner, and a water softener. In a time when changes are more rapid than ever, for me at least, one thing remains: my father-in-law's shovel, "Heat Treated Woods 2 Light Weight."

My father-in-law was a hard-driving, hard-working, opinionated Ohio farmer-preacher. I do not value all of his opinions, but I do value his shovel. And I'm grateful that he permitted me to marry his daughter. The shovel reminds me.

So be it.

Chapter 11

And so on . . .

In retirement, priorities change. With the help of Social Security, Mennonite Retirement Trust, and assorted savings, Mary and I have felt no need to work for wages. Maybe a few dollars here and there. Otherwise we are at ease. A good night's sleep is considered a victory of sorts.

Our tradition goes back to Jesus and beyond. It calls upon us to think large thoughts, not just small ones. The Jews were a cheeky little people who asserted that the Lord their God was not just a tribal deity but was the God of the whole earth and also the universe. Psalm 148 is said to have been written after the Jewish exile. It calls upon the world and the universe to praise the Lord.

Among those addressed are "Kings of the earth and all peoples, princes and rulers of the earth!"[53] After the exile the Jews had no king, so this little people, subject to the leaders of an empire, called upon the rulers of other nations to praise the Lord. It was a breakthrough in a time when each people typically had a god for themselves.

Having one Lord of the universe is a position that not everyone today is prepared to follow. The urge among some who aim to be religious is to try to turn the Lord into a tribal god. When politicians intone "God bless America," I get nervous because it sounds like tribalism.

There are those who respond with their own slogan, "God bless the whole world." It is the only way to go. We Mennonites are a little people, with less than two million members in the whole world. But we have tried to nourish a radical tradition, one that eschews violence and seeks to show love and concern for all.

We have no pope or tightly organized system, just little fellowships scattered about, where we read the Bible and encourage each other to be faithful.

As Appendix A reports, Mary and I have four sons, three daughters-in-law, nine grandchildren, and one great-grandson. I have not written in any detail about our sons, and I will not brag about our grandchildren. Any of our sons would be capable of writing for himself, and I would urge them do so.

When we consider our grandchildren, we are quite aware that we are blessed in a way that some couples are not. Our genes are passed on, and we hope that our faith is also passed on. The Christian story is one that each generation is in a position to accept, reject, or modify.

In Matthew 28 we read that after Jesus' resurrection, "the eleven disciples went to Galilee, to the mountain to which Jesus had directed them. When they saw him, they worshiped him, but some doubted."[54] From the account, it does not seem clear to me whether these doubts were cleared up by the appearance of Jesus. But we do know that a number of them got busy afterward and spread the good news.

Moriah Hurst wrote in *The Mennonite* about her experience in a ministry to young adults in Australia:

> In Australia's post-Christendom context, it is thoroughly uncool that I work for the church. . . .
>
> Inevitably I get, "How can you work for a church when you still have questions?"
>
> I explain: "I come from a tradition that works through community discernment. I prayed with others, heard a clear call to the work I am doing, and discerned that calling with a community of people willing to name my strengths and challenge me on my weaknesses."[55]

In 1991 I visited Moriah's family in Australia when she was a little girl. Now she is an adult, doing her part to tell the Christian story and encourage others to take it seriously. So the tradition of faith goes on, and we who are older take courage from the faith of the younger ones.

Meanwhile we have a concept passed on to us from the Jews—a belief in the resurrection from the dead. In Jesus' time this doctrine was accepted by the Pharisees but not by the Sadducees, as illustrated by an encounter Jesus had with a group of them reported in all three of the synoptic Gospels.

As Luke presents it, they told him a whopper joke about a woman who outlived seven husbands: "In the resurrection, therefore, whose wife will she be?"[56] In reply, Jesus did not quote from the Prophets or the Writings but from the Torah, which they claimed to accept. In the account of Moses at the burning bush, God is identified as the God of Abraham, Isaac, and Jacob. "Now he is God not of the dead, but of the living."[57]

The New Testament writers based their belief in the resurrection, however, on the resurrection of Jesus himself. All four of the Gospels include the account of the empty tomb. But Paul, writing to the Corinthians perhaps a decade earlier than the Gospel of Mark, faces the issue head-on. Evidently some sophisticates in Corinth have denied the idea of the resurrection. Paul insists that our faith rests on the resurrection of Christ.

Then he goes on to describe resurrection by using an analogy from the natural experience, the death and life of a seed: "What you sow does not come to life unless it dies." He continues from there to describe "a mystery": "We will not all die, but we will all be changed."[58]

Something in our culture does not like a mystery. Science is expected to solve mysteries, not leave them hanging. At some point we need to decide which way to go. J. Denny Weaver states it as follows: "The resurrection does not fit into the categories of knowing and testing in our known world, but the Bible speaks about resurrection, and it is the basis of our faith. I believe in the resurrection."[59]

We may have our doubts, but at some point we need to go one way or the other. Belief in the resurrection is a part of our tradition. At the end of his resurrection chapter, the apostle Paul urges the Corinthians to "be steadfast, immovable, always excelling in the work of the Lord, because you know that in the Lord your labor is not in vain."[60] I will go with Paul. And I wait to see what will happen.

Appendix A

Our family

Our sons are named in birth order. Grandchildren are listed in their birth order below their parents. These addresses are valid at the time of writing:

Dennis Hertzler, Monessen, Pa.

Ronald and Laurel Schmidt Hertzler, Telford, Pa.
    Brendon, Conshohocken, Pa.
    Bryce, Lansdale, Pa.
    Bethany, Harleysville, Pa.

Gerald and Mary DeCrane Hertzler, Goshen, Ind.
    Megan and Cameron Richmond, Indianapolis, Ind.
    Kaitlin and Kurtis Baumgartner, Westfield, Ind.
    Cohen Lee (great-grandson)

Daniel Mark and Christie Bradford Hertzler, Lancaster, Pa.
    Alicia and Zachary Hurst, Lancaster, Pa.
    Joshua, Salem, Ore.
    Abigail, Lancaster, Pa.
    Jacob, Lancaster, Pa.

Appendix B

Incomplete list of Mary's flowers

This is a not-quite-complete list of Mary's perennial flowers. Most are true perennials. Some reseed themselves.

Ageratum
Baby's Breath
Bachelor's Buttons
Bee Balm
Blue Grass
Brown-eyed Susan
Butterfly Bush
Butterfly Plant
Chrysanthemum
Clematis
Columbine
Coneflower
Coral Bells
Cornflower
Cosmos
Dahlia
Daisy
Daylily
Delphinium
Dianthus (Sweet William)
Dusty Miller
False Indigo
Flax
Fleabane
Forget-me-not

Foxglove
Globe Thistle
Grape Hyacinth
Hen and Chicks
Hosta (Plantain Lily)
Hyacinth
Iris (numerous varieties)
Lavender
Lilies (various)
Lily of the Valley
Narcissus
None-so-pretty (Catchfly)
Oriental Poppy
Peony
Phlox
Poppy
Primrose
Red Hot Poker (Fire Dance)
Rose (at least 12 varieties)
Rose Campion
Snow on the Mountain
Tulip
Veronica
Yarrow

Appendix C

Vehicles we have owned

A list of our automobiles, each with purchase year, approximate price, and extent of service:

1930 Marquette	$100	1948-52
1942 Studebaker	$295	1952-54
1947 Plymouth	$225	1954-57
1949 Plymouth	$125	1957-60
1953 Chevrolet	$300	1960-64
1961 Chevrolet	$1,200	1964-68
1964 Chevrolet	$1,200	1968-71
1967 Plymouth	$1,200	1971-76
1972 Dodge Colt	$900	1976-79
1980 Mazda GLC	$5,025	1979-88
1988 Mercury Tracer	$9,000	1988-92
1992 Honda Civic	$9,000	1992-2002
2002 Honda Civic	$15,000	2002-2009
2006 Toyota Corolla	$13,000	2009–

Also trucks:

1987 Toyota Pickup	$4,000	1991-2005
1997 Nissan Pickup	$3500	2005–

Notes

1. *Gospel Herald*, November 18, 1997, 6-7.
2. Daniel Hertzler, *A Little Left of Center* (Telford, Pa.: Pandora Press U.S., 2000).
3. Eric Hobsbawm and Antonio Polito, *On the Edge of the New Century* (New York: New Press, 2000), 162.
4. John Howard Yoder, *For the Nations* (Grand Rapids: Eerdmans, 1997), 244.
5. Farley Mowat, *And No Birds Sang* (Boston: Little, Brown, 1979), 218.
6. *Natural History* [magazine], July/August, 2003, 28-34.
7. Chris Hedges, *War Is a Force That Gives Us Meaning* (New York: Public Affairs, 2002), 3.
8. *Newsweek*, March 10, 2003, 13.
9. Howard Zinn, *A People's History of the United States: 1492–Present*, Harper Perennial Modern Classics (New York: HarperCollins, 2003), 109.
10. *The Good War and Those Who Refused to Fight It*, TV Documentary, Paradigm Productions, in association with the Independent Television Service, with funding provided by the Corporation for Public Broadcasting (2000, http://ibcoacet.typepad.com/blog/2012/07/download-the-movie-the-good-war-and-those-who-refused-to-fight-it-online.html).
11. Archbishop James Ussher, *Annals of the World* (first in Latin in 1654, then in English in 1658).
12. Ian Wilson, *Before the Flood* (New York: St. Martin's Press, 2001), 268.
13. Genesis 1:14 New Revised Standard Version. Unless otherwise specified, biblical quotations are from NRSV.
14. Judges 19:29.
15. John W. Miller, *How the Bible Came to Be* (New York: Paulist Press, 2004), 49, 50.
16. Proverbs 6:6 King James Version (KJV).
17. Stanley Hauerwas, *Unleashing the Scripture* (Nashville: Abingdon, 1993), 17.

18. Romans 12:11, KJV, NRSV.
19. Ellen F. Davis and Richard B. Hays, *The Art of Reading Scripture* (Grand Rapids: Eerdmans, 2003), xv, 12.
20. Matthew 5:44.
21. Mark I. Wallace, *The Second Naiveté* (Macon, Ga.: Mercer University Press, 1990), 119.
22. Nancey Murphy, *Anglo-American Postmodernity* (Boulder: Westview Press, 1997), 34.
23. First John 4:12, 15, 16b.
24 James William McClendon Jr., *Biography as Theology*, rev. ed. (Philadelphia: Trinity Press International, 1990), 144.
25. James William McClendon Jr., "The Radical Road One Baptist Took," *Mennonite Quarterly Review* 74 (October 2000): 507-8.
26. John Howard Yoder, *The Politics of Jesus*, 2nd ed. (Grand Rapids: Eerdmans, 1994), 28.
27. 1 Corinthians 1:23-24.
28. Joel B. Green and Mark D. Baker, *Recovering the Scandal of the Cross* (Downers Grove, Ill.: InterVarsity Press, 2000), 20.
29. John Driver, *Understanding the Atonement for the Mission of the Church* (Scottdale, Pa.: Herald Press, 1986).
30. Lamar Williamson Jr., *Mark*, Interpretation: A Bible Commentary for Teaching and Preaching (Atlanta: John Knox Press, 1983), 156-57.
31. Timothy Geddert, *Mark*, Believers Church Bible Commentary (Scottdale, Pa.: Herald Press, 2001), 212.
32. Menno Simons, *The Complete Writings of Menno Simons* (Scottdale, Pa.: Herald Press, 1956), 556.
33. Richard B. Hays, *First Corinthians*, Interpretation: A Bible Commentary for Teaching and Preaching (Louisville, Ky.: John Knox Press, 1997), 205.
34. John Howard Yoder, *Body Politics* (Scottdale, Pa.: Herald Press, 1992), 14.
35. Ibid., 26.
36. 1 Corinthians 1:23b-24.
37. Peter and Elfrieda Dyck, *Up from the Rubble* (Scottdale, Pa.: Herald Press, 1991).
38. Daniel Hertzler, *A Little Left of Center* (Telford, Pa.: Pandora Press U.S., 2000).
39. Ray Gingerich and Earl Zimmerman, eds., *Telling Our Stories* (Telford, Pa.: Cascadia Publishing House, 2006), 52.
40. Ephesians 4:11.
41. For Allegheny Mennonite Board: *Mennonite Yearbook and Direc-*

tory, 1962, 31; 1963, 31; 1964, 30; 1965, 33; 1966, 28; 1967, 29. For Goshen College Overseers: 1968, 14; 1969, 15; 1970, 19; 1971, 17; 1972, 51. For Mennonite Board of Education: 1974, 61; 1975, 89. For Allegheny Mennonite Conference: 1981, 39; 1982, 42; 1983, 40; 1984, 45; 1987-88, 46.

42. Membership figure from Allegheny Mennonite Conference office, Somerset, Pennsylvania.

43. Rodney Stark, *The Rise of the Christian Church* (Princeton: Princeton University Press, 1986).

44. Daniel Hertzler, *From Germantown to Steinbach* (Scottdale, Pa.: Herald Press, 1981).

45. See "Allegheny Mennonite Conference," in *Mennonite Yearbook and Directory, 1984-1991* (Scottdale, Pa.: Mennonite Publishing House, 1991).

46. William Alexander, *The $64 Tomato* (Chapel Hill, N.C.: Algonquin Books, 2006), 242-43.

47. Marcia Bonta, *Appalachian Spring* (Pittsburgh: University of Pittsburgh Press, 1991), 154.

48. Frederick Lewis Allen, *Only Yesterday* (New York: Perennial Classics, 2000), 135.

49. Ibid., 136.

50. Brian Ladd, *Autophobia* (Chicago: University of Chicago Press, 2008), 2.

51. Ibid., 186.

52. Alex Dubro, "The Myth of the Efficient Car," *The Progressive*, May 2009, 28-30.

53. Psalm 148:11.

54. Matthew 28:16-17.

55. *The Mennonite*, November 17, 2009, 10.

56. Luke 20:33a

57. Luke 20:38a.

58. 1 Corinthians 15:36-56.

59. Gingerich and Zimmerman, *Telling Our Stories*, 243.

60. 1 Corinthians 15:58.

The Author

Daniel Hertzler grew up near Elverson, a small town in Eastern Pennsylvania. He began at Eastern Mennonite College in 1947 and graduated with a ThB in 1962.

On July 12, 1952, he was married to Mary Yoder of Mantua, Ohio, and in September of that year they moved to Scottdale, Pennsylvania, where he began work as an editor at Mennonite Publishing House. In 1973 he became editor of *Gospel* Herald and then retired from that position in 1990.

Since January 1, 1957, Dan and Mary have had their home three miles from Scottdale along Jacobs Creek, the border between Fayette and Westmoreland Counties. The address has been changed twice and now is 321 Creek Road.

Dan finished his last committee assignment in 2011, but as of this writing continues as instructor for Unit 2, "The Biblical Story," in Pastoral Studies Distance Education. This is a five-unit college-level course in the study of pastoral work for students who do not find it convenient to travel to a seminary.

www.ingramcontent.com/pod-product-compliance
Lightning Source LLC
Chambersburg PA
CBHW022107040426
42451CB00007B/168